The B Cookbook

Low Calorie, Low Carbohydrates, No Added Salt Diet

by

Marion P Green

DORRANCE PUBLISHING CO
EST. 1920
PITTSBURGH, PENNSYLVANIA 15238

The contents of this work, including, but not limited to, the accuracy of events, people, and places depicted; opinions expressed; permission to use previously published materials included; and any advice given or actions advocated are solely the responsibility of the author, who assumes all liability for said work and indemnifies the publisher against any claims stemming from publication of the work.

All Rights Reserved
Copyright © 2019 by Marion P Green

No part of this book may be reproduced or transmitted, downloaded, distributed, reverse engineered, or stored in or introduced into any information storage and retrieval system, in any form or by any means, including photocopying and recording, whether electronic or mechanical, now known or hereinafter invented without permission in writing from the publisher.

Dorrance Publishing Co
585 Alpha Drive
Suite 103
Pittsburgh, PA 15238
Visit our website at www.dorrancebookstore.com

ISBN: 978-1-4809-5521-9
eISBN: 978-1-4809-5544-8

I am not a professional writer or chef. I am an overweight diabetic with CHF.

I have been collecting recipes for years. I have recently started adapting them to my dietary needs.

Since I started watching my intake of carbohydrates, sodium, and calories, I have lost twenty pounds and my B/P is normal again, all within two months.

I use regular food, unless specified, to make these dishes.

These recipes show that you can eat well and still take care of yourself.

I am on a fixed budget, so I use a lot of ingredients that could probably have fewer carbohydrates, sodium, or calories if bought them in the store.

Feel free to exchange ingredients to your taste and budget.

I want to thank all of the authors of the recipes I have collected and used.

I use calorieking.com for my intake calculations.

Good Luck,

Marion P Green

T. = TABLESPOON
t. = TEASPOON
c. = CUP
@ = AT
lb. = POUND(S)
oz. = OUNCE(S)
CAR = CARBOHYDRATE(S)
SOD = SODIUM
CAL = CALORIE(S)
SC = SLOW COOKER
Ct. = COUNT
PKG = PACKAGE

BACON = LOW-SODIUM BACON

CHOCOLATE CHIPS = SEMISWEET CHOCOLATE CHIPS UNLESS SPECIFIED

MILK = FAT-FREE (SKIM MILK) UNLESS SPECIFIED

PEANUT BUTTER IS CREAMY UNLESS SPECIFIED

EGGS ARE MEDIUM UNLESS SPECIFIED

FRUITS and VEGETABLES ARE FRESH EXCEPT CORN, MIXED VEGETABLES, and CHERRY PIE FILLING UNLESS SPECIFIED

FRUITS and VEGETABLES ARE MEDIUM UNLESS SPECIFIED

OIL = VEGETABLE OIL UNLESS SPECIFIED

MOZZARELLA CHEESE = PART-SKIM MILK

TORTILLA(S) = FLOUR TORTILLA UNLESS SPECIFIED

SUGAR = REGULAR GRANULATED WHITE SUGAR

SAUSAGE = PORK SAUSAGE

HONEY = HONEY SUBSTITUTE

PEPPER = GROUND BLACK PEPPER UNLESS SPECIFIED

CORN SYRUP = LIGHT UNLESS SPECIFIED

RECIPES

BEEF

BREAD

BREAKFAST

DESSERT

GLUTEN-FREE

GRILLED

HAMBURGER

HOLIDAY

MEXICAN

PARTY

PORK

POULTRY

SIDES

SLOW COOKER

SOUPS

HOMEMADE

BEEF

BALSAMIC SEASONED STEAK

☆ 1 lb. sirloin steak = SOD 187, CAL 536

☆ ¼ t. Pepper = CAL 1

☆ 2 T. balsamic vinegar (HOMEMADE) = CAR 4, SOD 1, CAL 17

☆ 2 t. steak sauce (HOMEMADE) = CAR 2, SOD 99, CAL 13

☆ 2 oz. Swiss cheese, cut into thin strips = CAR 3, SOD 40, CAL 215

Preheat broiler. Place steak on a broiler pan. Sprinkle with pepper. Broil 4 inches from heat for 7 min. Mix vinegar and steak sauce. Turn steak. Drizzle with 1 T. vinegar mixture. Broil just until meat reaches desired doneness. Remove steak to a cutting board. Let stand 5 min. Cut steak into ¼-inch slices. Return to broiler pan, arranging slices close together. Drizzle slices with remaining vinegar mixture. Top with cheese. Broil just until cheese is melted, 30 to 60 seconds.

WHOLE—4 SERVINGS	1 SERVING
CAR = 9	CAR = 2
SOD = 327	SOD = 82
CAL = 792	CAL = 199

BEEF IN CREAMY MUSHROOM SAUCE

- ☆ 2 T. cornstarch = CAR 15, SOD 1, CAL 61
- ☆ 1 c. water
- ☆ 1 lb. sirloin steak cut into thin strips = SOD 187, CAL 536
- ☆ 1 t. garlic, minced = 0
- ☆ 1/8 t. pepper = CAL 1
- ☆ 1 red bell pepper, chopped = CAR 6, SOD 6, CAL 46
- ☆ 3 c. mushrooms, sliced = CAR 4, SOD 11, CAL 46
- ☆ ¼ c. apple juice = CAR 7, SOD 2, CAL 29
- ☆ 1 beef bouillon cube = CAR 1, SOD 900, CAL 5
- ☆ 2 T. sour cream = CAR 1, SOD 14, CAL 56
- ☆ 2 T. Chives, chopped = CAL 2
- ☆ 3 c. macaroni, cooked = CAR 120, SOD 3, CAL 660

Combine cornstarch and water. Stir until dissolved, then set aside. Cook over medium-high heat, garlic and pepper until tender and aromatic. Add beef and bell pepper. Cook until meat is brown. Stir in mushrooms. Add apple juice and beef bouillon. Heat to boiling, then reduce to simmer and simmer 1 min. Pour in sour cream and cornstarch mixture. Stir until thickened. Stir in chives. Serve over macaroni.

WHOLE—8 SERVINGS	1 SERVING
CAR = 156	CAR = 20
SOD = 924	SOD = 116
CAL = 1442	CAL = 180

BEEF MIROTON

☆ 1 lb. roast, cooked = SOD 137, CAL 583

☆ 1 c. beef broth (HOMEMADE) = 0

☆ 1 c. beef gravy (HOMEMADE) = CAR 18, SOD 108, CAL 115

☆ 1 c. breadcrumbs (HOMEMADE) = CAR 48, SOD 511, CAL 276

☆ 5 T. butter, melted = SOD 455, CAL 510

☆ 1 ½ T. flour = CAR 9, CAL 42

☆ ½ T. rice vinegar = 0

☆ pepper to taste = CAL 1

Melt 2 T. butter. Stir in flour until you have a thick paste-like sauce. Pour in beef gravy, broth, and vinegar and mix until smooth. Add pepper to taste. Place a little of sauce on the bottom of baking pan. Layer meat on top. Pour the rest of the sauce over the top of the meat. Spread breadcrumbs over the top. Drizzle remaining butter over the top. Bake @ 400° for 5 to 10 min. or until warmed through and breadcrumbs are golden and crispy.

WHOLE—8 SERVINGS	1 SERVING
CAR = 75	CAR = 9
SOD = 1211	SOD = 151
CAL = 1527	CAL = 191

BEEF POTATO PEPPER SKILLET

☆   1 lb. roast, cut into chunks, cooked = SOD 137, CAL 583

☆   4 c. beef gravy (HOMEMADE) = CAR 72, SOD 431, CAL 459

☆   3 c. chunky-style hash browns, cooked = CAR 148, SOD 2700, CAL 1231

☆   1 red bell pepper cut into pieces = CAR 5, SOD 5, CAL 37

☆   1 green bell pepper cut into pieces = CAR 4, SOD 4, CAL 24

☆   1 c. water

☆   ¼ t. pepper = CAL 1

Combine all ingredients. Bring to a boil, stirring occasionally. Reduce heat.

Cover and simmer 12 to 14 min. or until peppers are tender.

WHOLE—8 SERVINGS	1 SERVING
CAR = 229	CAR = 29
SOD = 3277	SOD = 410
CAL = 2335	CAL = 292

BEEF STROGANOFF #1

☆ 6 T. butter = SOD 546, CAL 612

☆ 1 lb. sirloin steak, cut 1 in. wide 2 in. long = SOD 187, CAL 536

☆ 1 c. mushrooms, sliced = CAR 4, SOD 663, CAL 39

☆ pepper to taste = CAL 1

☆ 1/8 t. nutmeg = CAL 1

☆ ½ t. tarragon = CAL 1

☆ 1 c. sour cream = CAR 7, SOD 108, CAL 444

☆ 5 c. noodles, cooked = CAR 200, SOD 5, CAL 1100

Melt 3 T. butter in skillet. Brown steak over high heat, then remove meat and set aside. Melt last 3 T. Butter and cook mushrooms until tender and aromatic. Add tarragon and nutmeg and stir to combine. Add sour cream, thinning with water as necessary. Stir constantly. Add onion and steak back to pan. Simmer 2 min.
Serve over noodles.

WHOLE—8 SERVINGS	1 SERVING
CAR = 211	CAR = 26
SOD = 1509	SOD = 155
CAL = 2734	CAL = 342

BEEF TAPA

☆   1 lb. sirloin steak, sliced ½ in slices = SOD 187, CAL 536

☆   ¼ c. sugar = CAR 50, SOD 1, CAL 194

☆   ¼ c. brown sugar (HOMEMADE) = CAR 54, SOD 3, CAL 208

Combine sugars. Add steak and toss to combine, making sure meat is coated well. Put in airtight container and refrigerate for 24 hours. Fry steak over medium-high heat until browned.

WHOLE—8 SERVINGS	1 SERVING
CAR = 104	CAR = 13
SOD = 191	SOD = 24
CAL = 938	CAL = 117

BEEF WELLINGTON

- ☆ 2 ½lb. roast = SOD 342, CAL 1458
- ☆ ½ t. pepper = CAR 1, CAL 3
- ☆ 1 egg = SOD 62, CAL 63
- ☆ 1 T. water
- ☆ 1 T. butter = SOD 91, CAL 102
- ☆ 2 c. mushrooms, chopped = CAR 3, SOD 7, CAL 31
- ☆ 2 T. flour = CAR 12, CAL 56
- ☆ 1 puff pastry sheet = CAR 21, SOD 117, CAL 259

Sprinkle roast with pepper. Bake roast @ 425° for 30 min. Cover roast and refrigerate for 1 hour. Beat egg and water together. Heat butter. Add mushrooms to butter. Cook until liquid evaporates. Roll pastry sheet 4 inches longer and 6 inches wider than roast. Brush pastry with egg mixture. Spoon mushroom mixture onto pastry to within 1 inch of border. Place roast in center of pastry. Fold pastry over roast and press to seal. Place seam side down on baking pan. Tuck ends under to seal. Brush pastry with egg mixture. Bake @ 425° for 25 min. or until golden brown.

WHOLE—8 SERVINGS	1 SERVING
CAR = 37	CAR = 5
SOD = 619	SOD = 77
CAL = 1972	CAL = 247

BRAISED BEEF AND ROOTS

- ☆ 1 T. oil = CAL 120
- ☆ 2-lb. roast = SOD 274, CAL 1166
- ☆ 3 t. allspice = CAR 3, SOD 3, CAL 15
- ☆ 1 t. thyme = CAR 1, SOD 1, CAL 3
- ☆ 1 t. paprika = SOD 2, CAL 6
- ☆ ½ t. pepper = CAR 1, CAL 3
- ☆ 2 bay leaves = CAL 1
- ☆ 1 c. apple juice = CAR 28, SOD 10, CAL 114
- ☆ 3 c. beef broth (HOMEMADE) = 0
- ☆ 4 carrot sticks = CAR 2, SOD 19, CAL 11
- ☆ 3 potatoes, cubed = CAR 96, SOD 39, CAL 492
- ☆ 1 t. mustard = SOD 57, CAL 3
- ☆ 1 ½ T. water

Heat oil. Add roast to oil and cook until brown on all sides. Put roast in roasting pan. Add allspice, thyme, paprika, pepper, and bay leaf to pan roast is in. Pour in apple juice. Bring to a boil and cook for 3 min. Pour mixture over roast and cover. Bake @ 325° for 1 ½ hours. Remove roast. Remove bay leaves and discard. Add mustard, carrots, potatoes, and roast. Cover and bake for 1 hour more. Check vegetables to see if they are done. If not continue to cook in 20-min. increments until done.

WHOLE—8 SERVINGS	1 SERVING
CAR = 131	CAR = 16
SOD = 405	SOD = 51
CAL = 1934	CAL = 242

BREAD

BACON CRESCENT BUN

- ☆ 5 ¼ c. flour = CAR 483, SOD 16, CAL 2389
- ☆ ½ c. sugar = CAR 100, SOD 1, CAL 387
- ☆ 1 package yeast = CAR 1, SOD 4, CAL 23
- ☆ 1 c. milk = CAR 12, SOD 103, CAL 83
- ☆ ½ c. butter, cubed = SOD 727, CAL 810
- ☆ ½ t. caraway seeds = CAR 1, CAL 3
- ☆ 3 eggs = CAR 1, SOD 186, CAL 189
- ☆ 1 lb. bacon, cooked, crumbled = SOD 1320, CAL 692
- ☆ 1/8 t. white pepper = CAL 1
- ☆ 2 T. water

Combine 2 c. flour, sugar, and yeast. Heat milk and butter. Add milk mixture to flour mixture. Beat on medium speed for 2 min. Add caraway seeds and 2 eggs. Mix well. Stir in enough flour to make stiff dough. Knead on floured surface until smooth and elastic, about 6 to 8 min. Place in greased bowl, turning once to grease all sides. Cover and let rise in a warm place until doubled, about 1 hr. Combine bacon and pepper. Punch dough down when doubled. Put dough on lightly floured board. Divide dough in 4 portions. Roll each dough portion into a 12-inch circle. Cut circle in 12 wedges. Sprinkle a heaping t. of bacon mixture over each wedge. Roll each wedge from wide end. Place each wedge point down on a baking sheet 2 inches apart. Cover and let rise, 30 min. Beat water and remaining egg together. Brush egg mixture over rolls. Bake @ 350° for 12 to 14 min. or until golden brown.

WHOLE—48 SERVINGS	1 SERVING
CAR = 598	CAR = 13
SOD = 2357	SOD = 49
CAL = 4577	CAL = 95

BAKING POWDER BISCUIT

☆ 1 ¾ c. flour = CAR 161, SOD 4, CAL 796

☆ 1 T. baking powder = CAR 4, SOD 1463, CAL 7

☆ 1/3 c. butter = SOD 485, CAL 540

☆ ¾ c. milk = CAR 9, SOD 77, CAL 62

Mix flour and baking powder. Cut in butter until mixture resembles coarse crumbs. Add milk. Stir with fork until soft dough forms. Put on lightly floured surface. Knead 20 times or until smooth. Roll until dough is ½-inch thick. Cut with floured 2-inch cookie cutter to make 16 biscuits. Bake @ 450° for 10 min. or until golden brown.

WHOLE—16 SERVINGS	1 SERVING
CAR = 174	CAR = 11
SOD = 2026	SOD = 127
CAL = 1405	CAL = 88

BREAKFAST

BACON AND CHEESE QUICHE

- ☆ 1 pie crust = CAR 15, SOD 135, CAL 147
- ☆ 1 c. half-and-half (HOMEMADE) = CAR 6, SOD 194, CAL 111
- ☆ 4 eggs, slightly beaten = CAR 1, SOD 248, CAL 252
- ☆ ¼ t. pepper = CAL 1
- ☆ 8 slices bacon, crisply cooked, crumbled = SOD 660, CAL 346
- ☆ 1 c. cheddar cheese, shredded = CAR 1, SOD 702, CAL 455
- ☆ ¼ c. parmesan, shredded = SOD 76, CAL 22

Heat oven to 350°. Place pie crust in 9-inch pie pan. Mix half-and-half, eggs, and pepper. Set aside. Layer bacon and cheeses in crust. Pour egg mixture over top. Bake 40 to 50 min. or until knife inserted in center comes out clean. Let stand 5 min. Cut into wedges.

WHOLE—8 SERVINGS	1 SERVING
CAR = 23	CAR = 3
SOD = 2015	SOD = 252
CAL = 1334	CAL = 167

BREAKFAST BAKE

☆ dough for 8 crescent rolls = CAR 88, SOD 1760, CAL 800

☆ 1 c. ham, chopped = CAR 1, SOD 1723, CAL 186

☆ 6 eggs = CAR 1, SOD 372, CAL 378

☆ ½ c. milk = CAR 6, SOD 51, CAL 42

☆ ½ t. pepper = CAR 1, CAL 3

☆ 1 c. cheddar cheese, shredded = CAR 1, SOD 702, CAL 455

☆ 1 c. mozzarella cheese, shredded = CAR 4, SOD 737, CAL 341

Press dough on bottom of baking pan, firmly pressing holes and seams together to seal. Sprinkle ham over dough. Mix eggs, milk, and pepper together. Pour over ham. Top with cheeses. Bake @ 350° for 25 min. or until center is set.

WHOLE—12 SERVINGS	1 SERVING
CAR = 102	CAR = 9
SOD = 5345	SOD = 445
CAL = 2205	CAL = 184

BREAKFAST BURRITO

☆ 16 flour tortillas, warmed (HOMEMADE) = CAR 105, SOD 369, CAL 627

☆ 16 eggs, scrambled = CAR 1, SOD 992, CAL 1008

☆ 16 slices of bacon, cooked = SOD 1320, CAL 692

☆ 8 slices of American cheese, cut in half = CAR 18, SOD 2018, CAL 404

Place tortillas on individual pieces of plastic wrap. Place 1 slice of bacon down the middle of each. Divide eggs between tortillas, placing eggs on top of bacon. Place cheese slice halves down the middle over eggs. Roll tortilla up and wrap plastic wrap around it snugly. Eat then or freeze. If frozen microwave for 2 ½ min. or until heated and cheese is melted.

WHOLE—16 SERVINGS	1 SERVING
CAR = 124	CAR = 8
SOD = 4699	SOD = 294
CAL = 2731	CAL = 171

BREAKFAST CASSEROLE

☆ 1 c. green bell pepper, chopped = CAR 4, SOD 4, CAL 24

☆ 1 c. red bell pepper, chopped = CAR 5, SOD 5, CAL 37

☆ 6 eggs, beaten = CAR 1, SOD 372, CAL 378

☆ 1 c. milk = CAR 12, SOD 103, CAL 83

☆ ¾ c. cheddar cheese, shredded = CAR 1, SOD 526, CAL 342

☆ 1 t. Italian seasoning mix (HOMEMADE) = SOD 1, CAL 5

☆ ¼ t. pepper = CAL 1

☆ 4 slices bread, torn = CAR 48, SOD 511, CAL 276

Cook bell peppers for 4 min. or until crisp and tender. Mix eggs, milk, cheese, Italian seasoning, and pepper. Add to vegetables. Place bread in baking dish. Pour egg mixture over bread. Bake @ 350° for 45 to 50 min. or until knife comes out clean.

WHOLE—12 SERVINGS	1 SERVING
CAR = 71	CAR = 6
SOD = 1522	SOD = 127
CAL = 1146	CAL = 96

BREAKFAST COOKIES

- ☆ ½ c. pecans = CAR 3, CAL 377
- ☆ 3 c. oatmeal raisin cookie dough (HOMEMADE) = CAR 647, SOD 841, CAL 2816
- ☆ 1 c. carrots, shredded = CAR 8, SOD 76, CAL 45
- ☆ 1 c. wheat flake cereal, crushed = CAR 25, SOD 280, CAL 128
- ☆ ½ c. coconut = CAR 20, SOD 122, CAL 233
- ☆ 1 T. orange extract = 0
- ☆ ¾ t. cinnamon = CAR 1, CAL 5
- ☆ 1 ½ c. powdered sugar = CAR 180, SOD 4, CAL 700
- ☆ 2 t. orange juice = CAR 2, CAL 12

Preheat oven to 350°. Break up cookie dough. Add carrots, pecans, coconut, orange extract, and cinnamon. Knead until well blended. Divide dough into 12 equal portions. Place 6 on a cookie sheet and flatten to 2 ¾-inches round. Bake 14 to 17 min. or until edges are set and bottoms are golden brown. Cool on cookie sheet 3 min. Repeat with remaining dough. Combine powdered sugar and orange juice, blend well. Spoon glaze over cookies. Store in airtight container.

WHOLE—24 SERVINGS	1 SERVING
CAR = 886	CAR = 37
SOD = 1223	SOD = 51
CAL = 431	CAL = 180

BREAKFAST POTATOES

☆ 2 potatoes, sliced = CAR 65, SOD 26, CAL 328

☆ ¼ c. sliced onion = CAR 3, SOD 1, CAL 11

☆ 1/8 t. pepper = CAL 1

☆ ¼ c. cheddar cheese, shredded = SOD 175, CAL 114

Coat a 9-inch microwave-safe plate with cooking spray. Arrange potato and onion slices on plate. Sprinkle with seasonings. Cover and microwave on high 9 to 10 min. or until potatoes are tender, adding cheese in the last 30 seconds of cooking.

WHOLE—2 SERVINGS	1 SERVING
CAR = 68	CAR = 34
SOD = 202	SOD = 101
CAL = 454	CAL = 227

DESSERTS

BAKED APPLES

☆   6 apples, cored, halved = CAR 96, SOD 6, CAL 432

☆   2 c. orange-flavored soda = CAR 56, SOD 70, CAL 200

Arrange apples in baking pan. Pour soda over apples. Bake @ 350° until apples are tender.

WHOLE—6 SERVINGS	1 SERVING
CAR = 152	CAR = 25
SOD = 76	SOD = 13
CAL = 632	CAL = 105

BLUEBERRY LEMON SLAB PIE

☆ 2 refrigerated pie crusts = CAR 151, SOD 1870, CAL 1820

☆ 4 oz. cream cheese = CAR 3, SOD 336, CAL 396

☆ 1 ¼ c. lemon confit (HOMEMADE) = CAR 52, SOD 4, CAL 208

☆ 2 c. blueberries = CAR 35, SOD 3, CAL 169

Place pie crust 1 on top of the other and roll out to make a 16x13-inch rectangle. Place on ungreased cookie sheet. Fold in sides and crimp to form edges. Bake @ 450° for 10 min. or until golden brown. Cool 15 min. or until completely cooled. Mix cream cheese and lemon curd until fluffy. Spread lemon mixture over baked crust. Top with blueberries.

WHOLE—24 SERVINGS	1 SERVING
CAR = 241	CAR = 10
SOD = 2213	SOD = 92
CAL = 2593	CAL = 108

BROWNIE

☆ ¾ c. Nutella = CAR 108, SOD 75, CAL 1005

☆ 2 eggs = CAR 1, SOD 122, CAL 124

☆ 1/3 c. flour = CAR 31, SOD 1, CAL 152

Mix ingredients together. Put in baking pan. Bake @ 350° for 15 min. Let cool.

WHOLE—12 SERVINGS	1 SERVING
CAR = 140	CAR = 12
SOD = 198	SOD = 17
CAL = 1281	CAL = 107

GLUTEN-FREE

GLUTEN-FREE BANANA PANCAKES

☆ 1 ripe banana, sliced = CAR 24, SOD 1, CAL 105

☆ 2 eggs = SOD 124, CAL 126

Place eggs and banana in the blender. Blend until smooth. Heat a nonstick skillet. Spray the skillet with nonstick spray. Add the batter to the skillet in the shape of a pancake and space them out since they tend to spread. When bubbles start to form, flip it and cook for 10 seconds on the other side.

WHOLE—4 SERVINGS	1 SERVING
CAR = 148	CAR = 37
SOD = 125	SOD = 31
CAL = 231	CAL = 58

GRILLED

GRILLED BEEF FAJITA PACKS

☆ 1 lb. sirloin steak, cut into thin strips = SOD 290, CAL 830

☆ 1 green bell pepper, cut into ½-inch strips = CAR 3, SOD 3, CAL 18

☆ 1 red bell pepper, cut into ½-inch strips = CAR 4, SOD 2, CAL 24

☆ 1 yellow bell pepper, cut into ½-inch strips = CAR 2, SOD 1, CAL 11

☆ 1 onion, thinly sliced = CAR 10, SOD 3, CAL 48

☆ 8 t. fajita seasoning mix (HOMEMADE) = CAR 7, SOD 78, CAL 46

☆ 1/3 c. water

☆ 8 tortillas (HOMEMADE) = CAR 52, SOD 185, CAL 314

Heat gas or charcoal grill. Cut 4 (20x18-inch) sheets of heavy-duty foil. Mix beef, bell peppers, onion, seasoning mix, and water. Place ¼ of beef mixture in center of each foil sheet. Bring up 2 sides of foil over beef mixture so edges meet. Seal edges, making tight ½-inch fold. Fold again, allowing space for heat circulation and expansion. Fold other sides to seal. Place packets on grill over low heat. Cover grill and cook 13 to 18 min., rotating packets a ½-turn after about 6 min., until beef is cooked to desired doneness and peppers are tender. To serve, cut large "X" across top of each packet and carefully fold back foil to allow steam to escape. Serve beef mixture with tortillas.

WHOLE–8 SERVINGS	1 SERVING
CAR = 78	CAR = 10
SOD = 562	SOD = 70
CAL = 1291	CAL = 161

HAMBURGER

BEEF PIE

- ☆ 2 T. olive oil = CAL 240
- ☆ 1 lb. hamburger = SOD 340, CAL 1229
- ☆ 1/8 t. garlic powder = CAL 1
- ☆ 1 ½ c. beef gravy (HOMEMADE) = CAR 27, SOD 162, CAL 172
- ☆ 2 c. mixed vegetables = CAR 21, SOD 486, CAL 160
- ☆ 1 puff pastry sheet = CAR 21, SOD 117, CAL 259

Cook hamburger and garlic powder. Stir in gravy and vegetables. Pour into pie pan. Trim pastry to fit over pie pan. Bake @ 400° for 25 min. or until golden brown.

WHOLE—6 SERVINGS	1 SERVING
CAR = 69	CAR = 12
SOD = 1105	SOD = 184
CAL = 2061	CAL = 344

HOLIDAY

EASTER BREAKFAST—BACON EGG CHEESE BASKETS

☆ dough for 8 crescent rolls = CAR 88, SOD 1760, CAL 800

☆ 6 eggs = SOD 372, CAL 378

☆ pepper to taste = CAL 1

☆ ½ c. cheddar cheese, shredded = SOD 351, CAL 228

☆ 8 slices bacon = SOD 760, CAL 400

Separate dough into 8 triangles. Place each triangle in a muffin cup, pressing into bottom and around sides. Cut off excess dough. Fill in any spaces. Beat eggs. Add pepper. Cook eggs, scrambling until almost done. Divide between cups. Top each with 1 T. cheese. Bake @ 375° for 10 min. or until golden brown and cheese is melted. Cook bacon until done but not crisp. While still hot, bend in "U" shape. Let cool. Remove baskets from pan to serving platter. Place bacon handles on baskets.

WHOLE—8 SERVINGS	1 SERVING
CAR = 378	CAR = 47
SOD = 3243	SOD = 405
CAL = 1807	CAL = 226

MEXICAN

BEAN BURRITO BAKE

☆ 2 c. refried beans (HOMEMADE) = CAR 91, SOD 23, CAL 910

☆ 1 c. master mix (HOMEMADE) = CAR 96, SOD 1026, CAL 775

☆ ¼ c. water

☆ ¾ lb. hamburger, cooked = SOD 16, CAL 58

☆ 1 ½ c. cheddar cheese, shredded = CAR 2, SOD 1053, CAL 683

Mix together beans, master mix, and water. Spread mixture on bottom and halfway up the sides of a greased pie pan. Layer hamburger, then cheese. Bake @ 375° for 30 min.

WHOLE—8 SERVINGS	1 SERVING
CAR = 189	CAR = 24
SOD = 2121	SOD = 265
CAL = 2426	CAL = 303

BEAN AND CHEESE ENCHILADAS

☆ 2 c. kidney beans, cooked = CAR 58, SOD 4, CAL 450

☆ ½ c. water

☆ ½ c. salsa (HOMEMADE) = CAR 9, SOD 350, CAL 160

☆ 8 flour tortillas (HOMEMADE) = CAR 52, SOD 185, CAL 314

☆ ¼ lb. cheddar cheese brick, cut into 8 strips = SOD 352, CAL 229

☆ ¼ lb. cheddar cheese, shredded = SOD 351, CAL 228

SAUCE

☆ 2 c. tomato sauce (HOMEMADE) = CAR 49, SOD 88, CAL 1019

☆ ¼ t. pepper = CAL 1

☆ ½ t. garlic, minced = 0

☆ 1 t. chili powder = CAR 1, SOD 26, CAL 8

☆ ½ t. cumin = 0

Mix tomato sauce, pepper, garlic, chili powder, and cumin. Mash beans and liquid with salsa. Spoon bean mix down middle of tortilla. Place 1 stick of cheese down center of tortilla. Roll tortilla and place on baking pan seam side down. Pour sauce over tortillas. Sprinkle with shredded cheese. Bake @ 350° for 15 to 20 min. or until hot.

WHOLE—8 SERVINGS	1 SERVING
CAR = 169	CAR = 21
SOD = 1356	SOD = 170
CAL = 2409	CAL = 301

BEEF ENCHILADA CRESCENTS

☆ 1 lb. hamburger = SOD 340, CAL 1229

☆ 2 ½ c. enchilada sauce (HOMEMADE) = CAR 28, SOD 2331, CAL 178

☆ dough for 16 crescent rolls = CAR 176, SOD 3520, CAL 1600

☆ 4 c. cheddar cheese, shredded = CAR 5, SOD 2807, CAL 1822

☆ 1 c. tomatoes, diced = CAR 5, SOD 9, CAL 32

☆ 1 c. avocado, diced = CAR 2, SOD 11, CAL 240

Cook hamburger 5 to 7 min. Stir in ½ of the enchilada sauce and cook 5 min. Remove from heat and let stand for 5 min. Separate dough into 16 triangles. Place 2 T. of beef mixture on wide end of triangle, then roll up to point. Place each filled crescent into a baking dish. Pour remaining enchilada sauce over crescents. Top each crescent with ¼ c. of cheese. Bake @ 350° for 25 min. or until golden brown. Cool 5 min., then top each serving with diced tomatoes and avocados.

WHOLE—16 SERVINGS	1 SERVING
CAR = 216	CAR = 14
SOD = 9018	SOD = 564
CAL = 5101	CAL = 319

BEEF TACOS

- ☆ 2 t. oil = CAL 79
- ☆ 3 t. Garlic, minced = 0
- ☆ 1 t. cumin = 0
- ☆ 1 t. coriander = CAR 1, SOD 1, CAL 5
- ☆ ½ t. oregano = CAL 3
- ☆ ¼ t. cayenne pepper = CAL 1
- ☆ pepper to taste = CAL 1
- ☆ 1 lb. hamburger = SOD 340, CAL 1229
- ☆ ½ c. tomato sauce (HOMEMADE) = CAR 12, SOD 22, CAL 255
- ☆ ½ c. chicken broth (HOMEMADE) = 0
- ☆ 1 t. brown sugar (HOMEMADE) = CAR 2, CAL 9
- ☆ 2 t. cider vinegar = 0
- ☆ 10 taco shells = CAR 160, SOD 1196, CAL 1329
- ☆ 2 tomatoes, diced = CAR 5, SOD 9, CAL 33
- ☆ 1 c. lettuce, shredded = CAR 1, SOD 6, CAL 8
- ☆ 1 c. cheddar cheese, shredded = CAR 1, SOD 702, CAL 455
- ☆ ½ c. sour cream = CAR 4, SOD 61, CAL 246

Heat oil over medium heat. Add garlic, cumin, coriander, oregano, and cayenne pepper. Cook 1 min. Add hamburger until brown. Add tomato sauce, chicken broth, sugar, and vinegar, then bring to a simmer. Once liquid has reduced and thickened, about 10 min., taste and adjust with pepper. Serve in taco shells and top as desired.

(TOTALS INCLUDE A HELPING OF EACH OF THE TOPPINGS)

WHOLE—10 SERVINGS	1 SERVING
CAR = 186	CAR = 19
SOD = 2337	SOD = 234
CAL = 3653	CAL = 365

PARTY

BAKED MOZZARELLA BITES

☆ 1 crescent dough sheet = CAR 90, SOD 840, CAL 960

☆ 8 mozzarella sticks, cut crosswise into thirds = CAR 4, SOD 1600, CAL 432

☆ 3 T. butter, melted = SOD 273, CAL 306

☆ 2/3 c. seasoned breadcrumbs (HOMEMADE) = CAR 32, SOD 341, CAL 184

Heat oven to 375°. Unroll dough sheet and press into rectangle, 12x8 inches. Using pizza cutter, cut rectangle into 6 rows by 4 rows to make 24 2-inch squares. Place mozzarella stick in center of each rectangle, bring dough up and around cheese sticks, and press edges to seal. Place melted butter in small bowl. Place breadcrumbs in another small bowl. Dip each stick into butter and shake off excess. Roll in breadcrumbs to coat. Place about 1 inch apart on ungreased large cookie sheet. Bake 11 to 13 min. or until golden brown.

WHOLE—24 SERVINGS	1 SERVING
CAR = 126	CAL = 5
SOD = 3054	SOD = 127
CAL = 1882	CAL = 78

BASIL MUSHROOM TARTLETS

☆ 1 puff pastry sheet = CAR 21, SOD 117, CAL 259

☆ 1 T. butter = SOD 91, CAL 102

☆ 3 c. mushrooms, sliced = CAR 4, SOD 11, CAL 46

☆ 2 t. garlic, minced = 0

☆ 2 T. parmesan cheese, shredded = SOD 170, CAL 42

☆ 1 t. basil = CAL 4

Heat butter. Add mushrooms and garlic. Cook until tender and liquid has evaporated. Remove from heat. Stir in cheese and basil. Roll pastry into a 15x12-inch rectangle. Cut into 20 squares. Press the squares into muffin pan cups. Place 1 T. mushroom mixture into each cup. Bake @ 400° for 15 min. or until golden brown. Let cool in pan for 10 min.

WHOLE—20 SERVINGS	1 SERVING
CAR = 25	CAR = 1
SOD = 382	SOD = 19
CAL = 453	CAL = 23

BACON CHEESE DIP

☆ 3 slices bacon, cooked, crisp, chopped = SOD 285, CAL 150

☆ 8 oz. cream cheese = CAR 6, SOD 671, CAL 792

☆ ½ c. bbq sauce (HOMEMADE) = CAR 118, SOD 215, CAL 460

☆ ½ c. cheddar cheese, shredded = SOD 351, CAL 228

Set aside 2 T. of bacon. In food processor or blender, combine cheeses, bbq sauce, and bacon. Blend until well combined. Garnish with reserved bacon.

MAKES 1 ½ CUPS	3 T.	2 T.	1 T.
CAR = 124	CAR = 16	CAR = 10	CAR = 5
SOD = 1522	SOD = 190	SOD = 127	SOD = 52
CAL = 1630	CAL = 204	CAL = 136	CAL = 38

BROWN SUGAR CINNAMON CHEESECAKE DIP

☆ 8 oz. cream cheese = CAR 6, SOD 671, CAL 792

☆ ½ c. whipped topping (HOMEMADE) = CAR 13, SOD 281, CAL 334

☆ ½ c. brown sugar (HOMEMADE) = CAR 108, SOD 5, CAL 416

☆ 1 ½ T. cinnamon = CAR 3, SOD 3, CAL 27

☆ 1 T. nutmeg = CAR 2, SOD 1, CAL 37

☆ 1 t. vanilla = CAL 12

Whip cream cheese and whipped topping. Add brown sugar, cinnamon, nutmeg, and cinnamon. Continue to beat until smooth and creamy. Chill in refrigerator for 1 hr.

MAKES 1 ½ CUPS	3 T.	2 T.	1 T.
CAR = 132	CAR = 16	CAR = 10	CAR = 5
SOD = 961	SOD = 120	SOD = 80	SOD = 40
CAL = 1618	CAL = 202	CAL = 135	CAL = 67

BROWN SUGAR FRUIT DIP

☆ ½ c. brown sugar (HOMEMADE) = CAR 108, SOD 5, CAL 416

☆ 8 oz. cream cheese, softened = CAR 6, SOD 671, CAL 792

☆ 1 c. sour cream = CAR 9, SOD 122, CAL 492

☆ 1 t. vanilla = CAL 12

☆ 1 c. whipped topping (HOMEMADE) = CAR 25, SOD 562, CAL 668

Beat brown sugar and cream cheese until smooth. Add sour cream and vanilla, beating until smooth. Fold in whipped topping. Cover and chill for 4 hrs.

MAKES 1 ½ CUPS	3 T.	2 T.	1 T.
CAR = 148	CAR = 18	CAR = 11	CAR = 5
SOD = 1360	SOD = 170	SOD = 113	SOD = 57
CAL = 2380	CAL = 298	CAL = 198	CAL = 99

PORK

BACON PEPPER MACARONI AND CHEESE

☆ 3 c. macaroni, cooked = CAR 120, SOD 3, CAL 660

☆ 1/3 c. butter = SOD 485, CAL 540

☆ 1 c. red bell pepper, sliced = CAR 2, SOD 3, CAL 18

☆ ¼ c. green onion, sliced = CAR 1, SOD 4, CAL 8

☆ ¼ c. flour = CAR 23, SOD 1, CAL 114

☆ ¼ t. pepper = CAL 1

☆ 1 t. mustard = SOD 57, CAL 3

☆ 2 ¼ c. milk = CAR 27, SOD 259, CAL 371

☆ 10 slices bacon, cooked, cut into ½ in pieces = SOD 840, CAL 230

☆ 1 ¾ c. cheddar cheese, shredded = CAL 4, SOD 1210, CAL 342

☆ ¼ c. seasoned breadcrumbs (HOMEMADE) = CAR 12, SOD 128, CAL 69

Melt butter. Reserve 1 T. Add bell pepper and onion to butter and cook for 1 min. Stir in flour, pepper, and mustard. Gradually add milk. Stir constantly until mixture thickens, about 5 min. Stir in bacon and pasta. Remove from heat. Stir in cheese. Stir until cheese melts. Pour into baking pan. Stir breadcrumbs into reserved butter and drizzle over pasta mixture. Bake @ 350° for 20 to 25 min. or until edges are bubbly.

WHOLE—6 SERVINGS	1 SERVING
CAR = 189	CAR = 32
SOD = 2990	SOD = 498
CAL = 2356	CAL = 393

BAKED PASTA WITH MUSHROOMS, BACON, AND SPINACH

- ☆ 1 c. pasta, uncooked = CAR 60, SOD 4, CAL 312
- ☆ 1 ½ c. heavy cream (HOMEMADE) = CAR 14, SOD 843, CAL 905
- ☆ 4 slices bacon, chopped = SOD 380, CAL 200
- ☆ 2 c. onions, sliced = CAR 3, SOD 7, CAL 97
- ☆ ¼ t. pepper = CAL 1
- ☆ 3 c. mushrooms, sliced = CAR 4, SOD 11, CAL 46
- ☆ 1 c. spinach, drained = CAR 2, SOD 58, CAL 49
- ☆ ½ c. parmesan cheese, shredded = CAR 1, SOD 378, CAL 166
- ☆ 1 c. mozzarella cheese, shredded = CAR 6, SOD 1404, CAL 576

Heat oven to 350°. Spray 13x9-inch baking dish with cooking spray. Cook pasta as directed on package. Reserve ½ c. pasta cooking water. Drain pasta, return to pot. Add cream, toss. Set aside. Spray skillet with cooking spray, heat. Add bacon, cook until crisp. Remove bacon, set aside. Add onions and pepper to bacon drippings in pan, cook and stir 4 to 7 min. or until translucent. Add mushrooms, cook 6 to 10 min. longer or until browned and liquid evaporates. Add spinach and reserved pasta cooking water, cook and stir 1 min.

Pour mushroom mixture over pasta, toss to coat. Pour into baking dish. Top evenly with both cheeses. Cover dish tightly with foil. Bake 20 min. Remove foil, top with bacon. Bake uncovered 5 min. longer.

WHOLE—6 SERVINGS	1 SERVING
CAR = 90	CAR = 15
SOD = 3085	SOD = 514
CAL = 2352	CAL = 392

BISCUIT, HAM, AND POTATO BAKE

- ☆ 12-ct. biscuit dough (HOMEMADE) = CAR 348, SOD 3305, CAL 4023
- ☆ 2 eggs = SOD 124, CAL 126
- ☆ 1/3 c. milk = CAR 4, SOD 34, CAL 28
- ☆ ¼ t. dry mustard = SOD 15, CAL 1
- ☆ 1 c. potatoes, cubed = CAR 28, SOD 8, CAL 133
- ☆ ¼ c. onions, chopped = CAR 3, SOD 2, CAL 16
- ☆ ¼ c. green bell pepper, chopped = CAR 1, SOD 1, CAL 7
- ☆ ½ c. ham, diced = CAR 1, SOD 862, CAL 93
- ☆ ½ c. cheddar cheese, shredded = CAR 1, SOD 351, CAL 228

Beat eggs, milk, and mustard. Stir in potatoes, onions, bell pepper, ham, and cheese. Cut each biscuit into pieces and arrange evenly in baking pan. Pour egg mixture over biscuit pieces. Press down with back of spoon, making sure all biscuits are covered with egg mixture. Bake @ 350° for 40 to 45 min. or until edges are golden brown and center set. Let stand 5 min. before serving.

WHOLE—12 SERVINGS	1 SERVING
CAR = 386	CAR = 32
SOD = 4522	SOD = 377
CAL = 4655	CAL = 388

POULTRY

BAKED CHICKEN #1

☆ 8 pieces chicken = SOD 588, CAL 994

☆ 1 ½ c. buttermilk (HOMEMADE) = CAR 195, SOD 188, CAL 135

☆ 1 c. breadcrumbs (HOMEMADE) = CAR 48, SOD 511, CAL 276

☆ 1 t. rosemary = SOD 1, CAL 4

☆ 1 t. garlic powder = CAR 2, SOD 1, CAL 9

☆ ½ t. onion powder = CAR 1, SOD 1, CAL 4

☆ ½ t. pepper = SOD 1, CAL 3

Mix breadcrumbs, rosemary, garlic powder, onion powder, and pepper. Dip chicken in buttermilk. Roll in breadcrumb mixture. Place chicken on foil-covered baking pan. Bake @ 400° for 30 to 35 min. or until chicken is done.

WHOLE–8 SERVINGS	1 SERVING
CAR = 246	CAR = 31
SOD = 1291	SOD = 161
CAL = 1620	CAL = 203

BAKED CHICKEN #2

☆ 2/3 c. buttermilk (HOMEMADE) = CAR 87, SOD 83, CAL 60

☆ ¼ c. green onions, chopped = SOD 1, CAL 5

☆ 1 t. mustard = SOD 57, CAL 3

☆ 8 pieces chicken = SOD 588, CAL 994

☆ 1 c. breadcrumbs (HOMEMADE) = CAR 48, SOD 511, CAL 276

☆ ½ t. pepper = SOD 1, CAL 3

Whisk together buttermilk, chives, and mustard. Add chicken and allow to soak overnight or at least 30 min. Remove chicken from marinade and season with pepper. Discard marinade. Dip chicken in breadcrumbs. Place chicken in baking pan. Spray chicken with cooking spray. Bake @ 425° for 25 to 30 min.

WHOLE—8 SERVINGS	1 SERVING
CAR = 135	CAR = 17
SOD = 778	SOD = 97
CAL = 1341	CAL = 168

BAKED CHICKEN #3

☆ 8 pieces of chicken = SOD 588, CAL 994

☆ 1 ½ c. crackers, crushed = CAR 75, SOD 1172, CAL 442

☆ ¼ t. cayenne pepper = CAL 1

☆ 2 large egg whites = SOD 110, CAL 34

☆ 2 T. water

☆ 2 T. butter, melted = SOD 182, CAL 204

Combine cracker crumbs and cayenne pepper. Combine egg whites and water. Brush chicken with egg mixture. Sprinkle with crumb mixture and gently press into chicken. Place on baking pan. Drizzle with melted butter. Bake @ 375° for 45 to 55 min. or until chicken is done.

WHOLE—8 SERVINGS	1 SERVING
CAR = 75	CAR = 9
SOD = 2052	SOD = 257
CAL = 1675	CAL = 209

BBQ CHEESEBURGER PASTA

- ☆ 1 lb. ground chicken = SOD 365, CAL 729
- ☆ 2 c. hot water
- ☆ 4 c. milk = CAR 48, SOD 412, CAL 334
- ☆ 2 boxes cheeseburger macaroni = CAR 135, SOD 4860, CAL 660
- ☆ 1 c. cheddar cheese, shredded = CAR 1, SOD 702, CAL 455
- ☆ ½ c. bacon bits (HOMEMADE) = SOD 380, CAL 200
- ☆ ¼ c. bbq sauce (HOMEMADE) = CAR 109, SOD 109, CAL 505

Cook chicken for 5 to 7 min. or until cooked. Stir in hot water, milk, uncooked pasta, and sauce mix. Heat to boiling, stirring occasionally. Reduce heat. Cover and simmer for 5 min., stirring occasionally. Stir in cheese and ¼ c. bacon bits. Cover and simmer for 5 min. Remove from heat, uncover. Sprinkle remaining bacon bits and drizzle bbq sauce over top. Stir before serving.

WHOLE—12 SERVINGS	1 SERVING
CAR = 293	CAR = 24
SOD = 6828	SOD = 569
CAL = 2883	CAL = 240

BBQ CHICKEN CRESCENT

☆ dough for 8 crescent rolls = CAR 88, SOD 1760, CAL 800

☆ 2 chicken breasts, cooked, cut into 4 strips each = SOD 147, CAL 249

☆ 3 T. bbq sauce (HOMEMADE) = CAR 81, SOD 82, CAL 284

☆ 1/3 c. cheddar cheese, shredded = SOD 232, CAL 150

Heat oven to 350°. Spray cookie sheet with cooking spray. Separate dough into 8 triangles. Place 1 chicken breast strip on each triangle, top with sauce and about 1 t. cheese. Rollup loosely as directed on can. Place on cookie sheet. Sprinkle with remaining cheese. Bake 14 to 16 min. or until golden brown.

WHOLE—8 SERVINGS	1 SERVING
CAR = 169	CAR = 21
SOD = 2221	SOD = 278
CAL = 1483	CAL = 185

BBQ CHICKEN MACARONI AND CHEESE

☆ 6-oz. box macaroni and cheese = CAR 117, SOD 1410, CAL 660

☆ ¼ c. milk = CAR 3, SOD 26, CAL 21

☆ 2 T. bbq sauce (HOMEMADE) = CAR 54, SOD 54, CAL 189

☆ ½ c. chicken, cooked, diced = SOD 333, CAL 108

Cook macaroni and cheese according to directions and drain. Combine milk and bbq sauce in pot. Return to simmer, stirring until well combined. Add chicken and macaroni and cheese and warm through.

WHOLE—8 SERVINGS	1 SERVING
CAR = 174	CAR = 22
SOD = 1823	SOD = 228
CAL = 978	CAL = 122

BBQ CHICKEN PINWHEEL BAKE

☆ 2 c. chicken, shredded = SOD 1380, CAL 448

☆ ½ c. bbq sauce (HOMEMADE) = CAR 217, SOD 217, CAL 4758

☆ dough for 8 crescent rolls = CAR 88, SOD 1760, CAL 800

☆ ¾ c. cheddar cheese, shredded = CAR 1, SOD 526, CAL 342

Preheat oven to 400°. Stir together chicken and bbq sauce. Unroll dough and make 2 long rectangles. Overlap long sides to form large rectangles. Firmly press perforations and edges to deal. Spread chicken mixture over dough, leaving about ½ inch on 1 side. Top chicken with cheese. Starting with topped side, roll up dough toward uncovered edge, pinch seam to seal. Using sharp knife, cut roll into 8 slices. Place in 8-to-9-inch round pan. Bake 18 to 22 min. or until golden brown and centers of pinwheels are no longer doughy. Cool slightly 5 to 10 min. Serve warm.

WHOLE—8 SERVINGS	1 SERVING
CAR = 226	CAR = 28
SOD = 3883	SOD = 485
CAL = 6348	CAL = 794

BREADED CHICKEN WITH TOMATOES

- ☆ 4 chicken breasts = SOD 294, CAL 497
- ☆ ½ c. breadcrumbs (HOMEMADE) = CAR 24, SOD 256, CAL 138
- ☆ ¼ c. parmesan cheese, shredded = SOD 339, CAL 83
- ☆ ¼ t. pepper = CAL 1
- ☆ 1 T. oil = CAL 120
- ☆ 2 T. oil for frying = CAL 240
- ☆ 2 c. tomatoes, chopped = CAR 11, SOD 18, CAL 65
- ☆ 2 T. green onions, chopped = CAR 1, SOD 4, CAL 10
- ☆ 1 T. garlic, minced = 0
- ☆ 1 t. balsamic vinegar (HOMEMADE) = CAR 1, CAL 2

Between pieces of plastic wrap, place each chicken breast smooth side down. Gently pound with flat side of meat mallet or rolling pin until about ¼-inch thick. Mix breadcrumbs, cheese, and pepper. Coat chicken with crumb mixture, pressing to coat well on both sides. In skillet, heat 2 T. of oil. Cook chicken in oil 6 to 10 min., turning once, until golden brown on outside and no longer pink in center. Remove chicken from skillet, keep warm. To skillet, add remaining oil, tomatoes, onions, and garlic. Cook and stir 2 min. Stir in vinegar, cook 30 seconds longer. Serve over chicken.

(FRYING OIL COUNTS AS 1 CAL IN 1 SERVING TOTAL)

WHOLE—4 SERVINGS	1 SERVING
CAR = 35	CAR = 9
SOD = 911	SOD = 228
CAL = 1158	CAL = 290

SIDES

BAKED BEANS

☆ 2 slices bacon, crisp, crumbled = SOD 190, CAL 100

☆ 2 c. pork and beans = CAR 68, SOD 1680, CAL 440

☆ 2 T. brown sugar (HOMEMADE) = CAR 27, SOD 1, CAL 104

☆ 2 T. ketchup = CAR 10, SOD 320, CAL 40

☆ 2 t. mustard = SOD 114, CAL 7

Combine all ingredients in casserole dish. Bake @ 375° for 30 to 45 min. or until hot.

WHOLE—8 SERVINGS	1 SERVING
CAR = 105	CAR = 13
SOD = 2305	SOD = 288
CAL = 691	CAL = 86

BALSAMIC OVEN-ROASTED GREEN BEANS

☆ 1 ½ c. green beans = CAR 4, SOD 5, CAL 48

☆ 3 t. olive oil = CAL 360

☆ lemon pepper to taste = SOD 40

☆ pepper to taste = CAL 1

☆ garlic, minced to taste = 0

☆ 2 t. balsamic vinegar (HOMEMADE) = CAR 1, CAL 3

Preheat oven to 425°. Line a large baking sheet with foil. Place the green beans in a pile in the middle. Pour olive oil over the beans and mix them around so they are all coated. Season with lemon pepper, pepper, and garlic to taste. Spread beans across pan. Sprinkle balsamic vinegar over beans. Bake 10 min. Stir beans and then bake for another 5 to 10 min.

WHOLE—8 SERVINGS	1 SERVING
CAR = 5	CAR = 0
SOD = 45	SOD = 6
CAL = 452	CAL = 57

BEANS AND CARAMELIZED ONIONS

- ☆ 4 slices bacon = SOD 380, CAL 200
- ☆ 2 onions, cut lengthwise into ½-inch wedges = CAR 20, SOD 7, CAL 97
- ☆ 10 c. green beans = CAR 27, SOD 31, CAL 321
- ☆ 3 T. cider vinegar = 0
- ☆ 4 ½ t. brown sugar (HOMEMADE) = CAR 20, SOD 1, CAL 78
- ☆ ¼ t. pepper = CAL 1

Cook bacon until crisp. Reserve 2 T. drippings. Crumble bacon and set aside. Cook onion in bacon drippings until they are tender and golden brown, about 5 min. Stir vinegar and sugar into onions. Add beans to onions and cook uncovered over medium heat for 1 min., then add bacon. Toss gently. Season with pepper.

WHOLE–8 SERVINGS	1 SERVING
CAR = 67	CAR = 8
SOD = 419	SOD = 52
CAL = 697	CAL = 87

BROCCOLI AND APPLE SALAD

- ☆ 3 c. broccoli = CAR 11, SOD 90, CAL 93
- ☆ 3 apples, chopped = CAR 42, SOD 4, CAL 195
- ☆ ½ c. mixed dried fruit, chopped = CAR 64, SOD 20, CAL 276
- ☆ 1 t. onion, chopped = CAL 1
- ☆ ½ c. plain yogurt = CAR 4, SOD 43, CAL 67
- ☆ 4 slices bacon, cooked, crumbled = SOD 380, CAL 200

Combine broccoli, apples, dried fruit, and onion. Add yogurt, toss to coat. Sprinkle with bacon. Refrigerate until serving.

WHOLE—10 SERVINGS	1 SERVING
CAR = 121	CAR = 12
SOD = 537	SOD = 54
CAL = 832	CAL = 83

SLOW COOKER

SC BEEF BOURGUIGNON

- ☆ 6 bacon cooked, diced, save grease = SOD 810, CAL 222
- ☆ 3 lbs. stew meat = SOD 410, CAL 1750
- ☆ 3 carrots, diced = CAR 12, SOD 39, CAL 75
- ☆ pepper to taste = CAR 1, CAL 3
- ☆ 2 T. flour = CAR 12, CAL 56
- ☆ 3 c. tomato juice = CAR 27, SOD 1962, CAL 123
- ☆ 3 c. beef broth (HOMEMADE) = 0
- ☆ 1 T. tomato paste = CAR 2, SOD 16, CAL 13
- ☆ 2 t. garlic, minced = 0
- ☆ ½ t. thyme = CAL 1
- ☆ 1 bay leaf, crumbled = CAL 1
- ☆ 20 pearl onions = CAR 40, SOD 540, CAL 140
- ☆ 4 t. parsley, 1 bay leaf, and ¼ t. thyme tied in cheesecloth = SOD 8, CAL 6
- ☆ 3 c. mushrooms, sliced = CAR 4, SOD 11, CAL 46

Pat dry stew meat. Sprinkle with flour and pepper. Sear ¼ meat in 1/5 bacon grease, about 1 to 3 min. Put meat in slow cooker. Pour 1/5 c. of tomato juice into pan when finished with meat. Stir juice to get all brown pieces left behind, then add to slow cooker. Repeat steps until meat is gone. Add 1/5 of grease to pan and fry the carrots until softened. Add 1/5 of grease to pan and fry garlic and tomato paste until fragrant. Transfer the vegetable mixture to the slow cooker. Add last of grease to pan and fry mushrooms until they release all their liquid and the liquid has evaporated. Mushrooms should end up golden brown, about 8 to 10 min. Set aside. Stir ingredients in slow cooker and add thyme and bay leaf. Add herbs tied in cheesecloth. Add beef broth and remaining tomato juice. Cook on low for 6 to 8 hrs. Stir in bacon, pearl onions, and mushrooms. Cook on high for 10 min. Remove herbs in cheesecloth before serving.

WHOLE—8 SERVINGS	1 SERVING
CAR = 100	CAR = 13
SOD = 3796	SOD = 475
CAL = 2436	CAL = 305

SC BEEF CASSEROLE

☆ 1 ½ lbs. stewing meat = SOD 205, CAL 875

☆ 2 c. beef broth (HOMEMADE) = 0

☆ 2 T. flour = CAR 12, CAL 56

☆ 2 T. olive oil = SOD 1, CAL 239

☆ 3 carrots, chopped into 1-inch pieces = CAR 12, SOD 126, CAL 75

☆ 2 celery stalks, chopped = CAR 1, SOD 64, CAL 13

☆ pepper to taste = CAL 1

Combine beef, flour, and pepper. Heat oil in skillet until very hot. Add meat and brown on all sides, then remove and set aside. In slow cooker, layer carrots and beef. Add beef broth. Cook on high for 30 min., then on low for 6 to 8 hrs.

WHOLE—8 SERVINGS	1 SERVING
CAR = 25	CAR = 3
SOD = 396	SOD = 50
CAL = 1259	CAL = 157

SC BEEF ON RICE

- ☆ 2 lbs. stew meat = SOD 274, CAL 1166
- ☆ 4 c. beef broth (HOMEMADE) = 0
- ☆ 1 onion, chopped = CAR 8, SOD 4, CAL 44
- ☆ 1 t. Italian seasoning mix = (HOMEMADE) = SOD 1, CAL 5
- ☆ 1 t. pepper = CAR 1, SOD 1, CAL 6
- ☆ ¼ c. cold water
- ☆ 3 T. cornstarch = CAR 21, CAL 90
- ☆ 4 c. rice, cooked = CAR 195, CAL 967

Add beef broth and chopped onions to slow cooker. Sprinkle with pepper and Italian seasoning. Cover and cook on low for 8 hrs. or on high for 4 hrs. About 10 to 15 min. before serving, transfer slow cooker contents to a large stock pot and bring to a boil. Whisk together cold water and corn starch, add to pot, and stir until thickened. Serve over rice.

WHOLE—8 SERVINGS	1 SERVING
CAR = 2025	CAR = 28
SOD = 280	SOD = 35
CAL = 2278	CAL = 285

SC BEEF ROAST AND VEGETABLES

☆ 2-lb. roast = SOD 274, CAL 1166

☆ pepper to taste = CAL 1

☆ 1 onion, sliced = CAR 1, SOD 1, CAL 6

☆ 4 carrots, cut = CAR 16, SOD 168, CAL 100

☆ 4 potatoes, cut = CAR 120, SOD 32, CAL 568

☆ ½ c. water

Place roast into slow cooker. Add pepper. Place vegetables around roast. Add water. Cook on low 9 to 10 hrs. or high 5 to 6 hrs.

WHOLE—8 SERVINGS	1 SERVING
CAR = 137	CAR = 17
SOD = 475	SOD = 59
CAL = 1841	CAL = 230

SC BEEF STROGANOFF #2

☆ 1 lb. sirloin steak, cut into ¼-in. thick slices = SOD 187, CAL 536

☆ 2 t. parsley = SOD 3, CAL 1

☆ 2 T. mustard = CAR 1, SOD 341, CAL 20

☆ ½ t. dill weed = SOD 1, CAL 1

☆ ½ t. pepper = CAR 1, CAL 3

☆ 2 c. mushrooms, sliced = CAR 3, SOD 7, CAL 31

☆ 2 t. Worcestershire sauce (HOMEMADE) = CAR 2, SOD 2, CAL 8

☆ 3 t. garlic, minced = 0

☆ 1/3 c. flour = CAR 31, SOD 1, CAL 152

☆ 1 c. beef broth (HOMEMADE) = 0

☆ 2 T. cream cheese = CAR 1, SOD 106, CAL 99

☆ 1 c. sour cream = CAR 7, SOD 108, CAL 444

☆ 4 c. noodles, cooked = CAR 160, SOD 32, CAL 876

Place steak, parsley, mustard, dill, pepper, mushrooms, and garlic in slow cooker. Stir well. Combine flour, Worcestershire sauce, and broth. Add to slow cooker, then stir well. Cook on high for 1 hr. Reduce heat to low and cook for 7 to 8 hrs. or until steak is tender. Before serving stir in cream cheese and cook on high for 10 min. Stir in sour cream. Serve over noodles.

WHOLE—8 SERVINGS	1 SERVING
CAR = 206	CAR = 26
SOD = 788	SOD = 99
CAL = 2171	CAL = 271

SC BEEF STROGANOFF #3

- ☆ 1 ½ lb. stew meat = SOD 205, CAL 875
- ☆ ½ large onion, chopped = CAR 6, SOD 3, CAL 30
- ☆ 3 T. garlic, minced = 0
- ☆ 1 ¼ c. sliced mushrooms = CAR 2, SOD 4, CAL 19
- ☆ 1¼ c. beef broth (HOMEMADE) = 0
- ☆ ¼ c. soy sauce (HOMEMADE) = CAR 2, SOD 1, CAL 11
- ☆ ¼ c. red wine vinegar = 0
- ☆ ½ t. onion powder = CAR 1, SOD 1, CAL 4
- ☆ ½ t. garlic powder = CAR 1, SOD 1, CAL 5
- ☆ ½ c. coconut milk = CAR 4, SOD 23, CAL 38
- ☆ 3 T. cornstarch = CAR 2, CAL 90
- ☆ 2 T. water
- ☆ pepper to taste = CAL 1
- ☆ 6 c. noodles = CAR 228, SOD 48, CAL 1314

Place beef inside slow cooker and top with onions, mushrooms, and garlic. Mix together broth, soy sauce, vinegar, onion powder, and garlic powder. Pour on top of beef and vegetables. Set slow cooker to low and cook for 5 hrs. At the 5-hr. mark, add coconut cream. Mix together cornstarch and water. Add to slow cooker. Let simmer for another 30 min. to 1 hr. or until sauce is thickened and beef is tender. Serve over rice.

WHOLE—8 SERVINGS	1 SERVING
CAR = 246	CAR = 31
SOD = 286	SOD = 36
CAL = 2387	CAL = 298

SC BRISKET

☆ 4-lb. beef brisket = SOD 739, CAL 2302

☆ 1 bay leaf = CAL 1

☆ 1 ½ c. apple juice = CAR 41, SOD 15, CAL 171

☆ 1 t. garlic, minced = 0

☆ ½ t. thyme = CAL 1

☆ ¼ t. pepper = CAL 1

☆ 2 T. cornstarch = CAR 14, CAL 60

☆ 2 T. cold water

Put bay leaf in slow cooker. Add meat. Combine apple juice, sugar, garlic, thyme, and pepper, then pour over meat. Cook on low for 10 to 12 hrs. or on high 5 to 6 hrs. Remove meat and keep warm. Remove bay leaf and throw away. Remove 2 ½ c. of liquid. Combine cornstarch and water, then stir in cooking liquid and cook over medium heat until thickened. Cook and stir 2 more min. Serve meat with onion gravy.

WHOLE—16 SERVINGS	1 SERVING
CAR = 55	CAR = 3
SOD = 754	SOD = 47
CAL = 2536	CAL = 159

SC BBQ PULLED PORK FAJITAS

☆ 2 ½ lb. pork roast = SOD 635, CAL 1860

☆ 2 c. bbq sauce (HOMEMADE) = CAR 869, SOD 869, CAL 3031

☆ 1 T. chili powder = CAR 2, SOD 76, CAL 24

☆ 1 t. cumin = 0

☆ ½ c. green bell pepper = CAR 2, SOD 2, CAL 15

☆ ½ c. red bell pepper = CAR 3, SOD 1, CAL 19

☆ 18 flour tortillas (HOMEMADE) = CAR 118, SOD 415, CAL 705

Put roast in slow cooker. Mix bbq sauce, chili powder, and cumin, then pour over roast. Cook on low for 8 to 10 hrs. Remove roast using 2 forks, shred meat, and return to slow cooker. Stir in bell peppers. Increase heat to high and cook for 30 min. or until mixture is hot and vegetables are tender. Serve ½ c. meat mixture in each tortilla.

WHOLE—18 SERVINGS	1 SERVING
CAR = 994	CAR = 55
SOD = 1998	SOD = 111
CAL = 5654	CAL = 314

SC BEEF BURRITOS

☆ 2-lb. brisket = SOD 635, CAL 1978

☆ 1 T. oil = CAL 120

☆ 2 green bell peppers, chopped = CAR 7, SOD 7, CAL 46

☆ 8 flour tortillas (HOMEMADE) = CAR 52, SOD 185, CAL 314

☆ 1 c. pasta sauce (HOMEMADE) = CAR 11, SOD 32, CAL 155

☆ ½ c. beef broth (HOMEMADE) = 0

☆ 3 t. garlic, minced = 0

Heat oil in skillet and brown meat. Put meat in slow cooker. Cook green pepper in same skillet for about 4 min. or until tender. Put green pepper in slow cooker. Add pasta sauce, beef broth, and garlic to slow cooker. Cook on low for 4 to 6 hrs. or until meat is tender. Remove meat from slow cooker and let rest 5 min. Shred with 2 forks, then return to slow cooker. Serve wrapped in tortillas.

WHOLE—8 SERVINGS	1 SERVING
CAR = 70	CAR = 9
SOD = 859	SOD = 107
CAL = 2613	CAL = 327

SC BBQ PORK ROAST WITH CARROTS

☆ 1 ½ pork roast = SOD 280, CAL 819

☆ ½ c. bbq sauce (HOMEMADE) = CAR 217, SOD 217, CAL 4758

☆ 2 T. honey (HOMEMADE) = CAR 125, SOD 2, CAL 484

☆ 1 T. balsamic vinegar (HOMEMADE) = CAR 2, SOD 1, CAL 9

☆ 1 T. soy sauce (HOMEMADE) = CAL 3

☆ ½ t. ginger = CAR 1, CAL 3

☆ ¼ t. pepper = CAL 1

☆ 2 ½ c. honey-glazed carrots (HOMEMADE) = CAR 192, SOD 369, CAL 1079

Put roast in slow cooker. Stir together bbq sauce, honey, vinegar, soy sauce, ginger, and pepper, then pour over roast. Cook on low for 6 to 7 hrs. Place carrots around roast. Increase heat to high and cook for 30 min.

WHOLE—8 SERVINGS	1 SERVING
CAR = 438	CAR = 55
SOD = 867	SOD = 108
CAL = 2858	CAL = 357

SC BACON, RANCH, CHICKEN, AND PASTA

- ☆ 6 pieces chicken, cooked, shredded = SOD 2544, CAL 826
- ☆ 6 slices of bacon, cooked and diced = SOD 494, CAL 260
- ☆ 3 t. garlic, minced = 0
- ☆ 4 T. dry ranch dressing mix (HOMEMADE) = CAR 21, SOD 72, CAL 135
- ☆ 1 ½ c. condensed cream of chicken soup (HOMEMADE) = CAR 28, SOD 640, CAL 366
- ☆ 1 c. sour cream = CAR 7, SOD 108, CAL 444
- ☆ ½ t. pepper = CAR 1, CAL 3
- ☆ ½ c. water
- ☆ 1 c. spaghetti, cooked = CAR 40, SOD 1, CAL 220

Place chicken in slow cooker. Mix bacon, garlic, ranch dressing mix, soup, sour cream, pepper, and water. Pour over chicken. Cook on low for 6 hrs. or high for 3 to 4 hrs. Shred chicken and toss creamy chicken mixture with spaghetti.

WHOLE—12 SERVINGS	1 SERVING
CAR = 57	CAR = 5
SOD = 3859	SOD = 322
CAL = 2254	CAL = 188

SC BACON CORN CHOWDER

☆ 1 lb. potatoes, cut into 1-inch cubes = CAR 69, SOD 27, CAL 349

☆ ½ c. onion, chopped = CAR 7, SOD 2, CAL 34

☆ 3 c. corn = CAR 82, SOD 1053, CAL 399

☆ 3 c. chicken broth (HOMEMADE) = 0

☆ ½ t. pepper = CAL 1

☆ 2 c. half-and-half (HOMEMADE) = CAR 12, SOD 388, CAL 221

☆ 2 T. cornstarch = CAR 14, CAL 60

☆ ½ lb. bacon, cooked, crumbled = SOD 2155, CAL 1134

In slow cooker, mix potatoes, onion, corn, broth, and pepper. Cover, cook on high 3 to 4 hrs. or until potatoes are tender. Beat half-and-half and cornstarch with whisk until smooth. Stir half-and-half mixture and bacon into corn mixture. Cover, cook 10 to 15 min. longer or until slightly thickened.

WHOLE—6 SERVINGS	1 SERVING
CAR = 184	CAR = 31
SOD = 3625	SOD = 604
CAL = 2198	CAL = 366

SC BEEF WITH MUSHROOMS STEW

- ☆ 12 potatoes cut in ¼ = CAR 290, SOD 122, CAL 1469
- ☆ ½ c. onion, chopped = CAR 6, SOD 2, CAL 32
- ☆ 1 c. baby carrots = CAR 14, SOD 177, CAL 79
- ☆ ½ c. mushrooms, sliced = CAR 1, SOD 2, CAL 8
- ☆ 1 ½ c. tomatoes, diced = CAR 7, SOD 14, CAL 49
- ☆ 1 ¼ c. beef broth (HOMEMADE) = 0
- ☆ ½ c. flour = CAR 46, SOD 1, CAL 228
- ☆ 1 T. Worcestershire sauce (HOMEMADE) = CAR 3, SOD 3, CAL 12
- ☆ 1 t. sugar = CAR 4, CAL 16
- ☆ 1 t. marjoram = CAL 2
- ☆ ¼ t. pepper = CAL 1
- ☆ 1 lb. stew meat = SOD 172, CAL 735

In slow cooker, mix all ingredients except beef. Add beef. Cover, cook on low 8 to 9 hrs. Stir well before serving.

WHOLE–8 SERVINGS	1 SERVING
CAR = 371	CAR = 46
SOD = 493	SOD = 62
CAL = 2631	CAL = 329

SC BEEF STEW #1

- ☆ 2 carrots, thinly sliced = CAR 9, SOD 84, CAL 50
- ☆ 2 potatoes, cut into ½-in. chunks = CAR 60, SOD 17, CAL 284
- ☆ 1 c. green beans = CAR 8, SOD 7, CAL 34
- ☆ 1 lb. stew meat = SOD 137, CAL 583
- ☆ 1 bay leaf = CAL 1
- ☆ 1 t. thyme = CAR 1, SOD 1, CAL 3
- ☆ 1 t. garlic, minced = 0
- ☆ 3 c. beef broth (HOMEMADE) = 0
- ☆ 2 T. brown sugar (HOMEMADE) = CAR 27, SOD 1, CAL 104
- ☆ 2 t. Worcestershire sauce (HOMEMADE) = CAR 2, SOD 2, CAL 8
- ☆ pepper to taste = CAL 1
- ☆ 3 T. flour = CAR 18, CAL 84
- ☆ 2 t. tomato paste = CAR 2, SOD 11, CAL 9

Put all ingredients except for flour and tomato paste into slow cooker and stir to combine. Cook on low 8 to 9 hrs. or high 4 to 5 hrs. or until meat and potatoes are tender. Thirty min. before serving, transfer a ladleful of broth to a small bowl. Add flour and tomato paste. Stir until smooth. Stir back into stew and cook for remaining ½-hr. Remove bay leaf before serving.

WHOLE—8 SERVINGS	1 SERVING
CAR = 126	CAR = 16
SOD = 260	SOD = 33
CAL = 1161	CAL = 145

SC BEEF STEW #2

☆ 2 lb. stew meat = SOD 274, CAL 166

☆ 2 T. olive oil = SOD 1, CAL 239

☆ 2 c. beef broth (HOMEMADE) = 0

☆ 12 slices bacon, cooked, crisp, crumbled = SOD 1620, CAL 444

☆ 2 c. tomatoes, diced = CAR 10, SOD 18, CAL 65

☆ 1/8 c. red bell pepper, chopped = CAR 1, SOD 1, CAL 6

☆ 1/8 c. green bell pepper, chopped = CAR 1, SOD 1, CAL 4

☆ ½ c. mushrooms, sliced = CAR 1, SOD 2, CAL 8

☆ ¼ c. celery, chopped = CAR 1, SOD 20, CAL 4

☆ ¼ c. carrot, chopped = CAR 2, SOD 22, CAL 13

☆ 4 t. garlic, minced = 0

☆ 2 T. tomato paste = CAR 5, SOD 32, CAL 27

☆ 2 T. Worcestershire sauce (HOMEMADE) = CAR 6, SOD 5, CAL 24

☆ 1 ½ t. pepper = CAR 1, SOD 1, CAL 9

☆ 1 t. garlic powder = CAR 2, SOD 2, CAL 10

☆ 1 t. onion powder = CAR 2, SOD 2, CAL 8

☆ 1 t. oregano = CAR 1 CAL 3

Heat oil. Add beef to oil and brown on all sides. Put beef in slow cooker. Add all other ingredients to slow cooker. Cook on low 6 to 8 hrs.

WHOLE–8 SERVINGS	SERVING
CAR = 33	CAR = 4
SOD = 2001	SOD = 250
CAL = 1030	CAL = 129

SC BEEF STEW #3

☆ 1 lb. stew meat = SOD 172, CAL 735

☆ ¼ c. flour = CAR 23, SOD 1, CAL 114

☆ 1 T. olive oil = CAL 120

☆ 4 potatoes, diced = CAR 130, SOD 51, CAL 656

☆ 4 carrots, chopped = CAR 21, SOD 209, CAL 124

☆ 1 onion, chopped = CAR 13, SOD 5, CAL 64

☆ 2 T. Garlic, minced = 0

☆ 1 bay leaf = CAL 1

☆ 2 t. pepper = CAR 3, SOD 2, CAL 12

☆ 2 c. beef broth (HOMEMADE) = 0

☆ 1 T. Worcestershire sauce (HOMEMADE) = CAR 3, SOD 3, CAL 12

☆ pepper to taste = CAL 1

Add beef to flour. Stir to coat. Heat olive oil in a skillet. Add beef and cook until browned, stirring as needed. Place meat in slow cooker. Add potatoes, carrots, onion, and garlic to the slow cooker with the bay leaf. Sprinkle the pepper on top and pour broth and Worcestershire sauce into the slow cooker. Cook on low 10 to 12 hrs. or high 6 to 7 hrs. Remove the bay leaf, stir well, and add pepper as needed before serving.

WHOLE—10 SERVINGS	1 SERVING
CAR = 193	CAR = 19
SOD = 443	SOD = 44
CAL = 1949	CAL = 195

SC BUFFALO CHICKEN DIP

☆ 16 oz. cream cheese = CAR 12, SOD 1343, CAL 1583

☆ 2 c. cheddar cheese, shredded = CAR 2, SOD 1403, CAL 911

☆ 1 c. ranch dressing (HOMEMADE) = CAR 12, SOD 745, CAL 1135

☆ 1 c. mozzarella cheese, shredded = CAR 6, SOD 1404, CAL 325

☆ ½ c. cheddar cheese, shredded = SOD 351, CAL 228

Mix cream cheese, 1 c. chicken, and ½ c. ranch dressing. Top with remaining chicken and ranch dressing. Sprinkle mozzarella cheese and cheddar cheese. Cook on low 2 hrs.

MAKES—4 CUPS	3 T.	2 T.	1 T.
CAR = 32	CAR = 2	CAR = 1	CAR = 1
SOD = 5246	SOD = 245	SOD = 164	SOD = 82
CAL = 4182	CAL = 196	CAL = 131	CAL = 65

SOUPS

BEAN SOUP

☆ 5 c. pinto beans, cooked = CAR 147, SOD 9, CAL 1223

☆ 8 c. water

☆ 1 c. ham, chopped = CAR 4, SOD 2666, CAL 239

☆ 3 c. carrots, chopped = CAR 10, SOD 105, CAL 62

☆ pepper to taste = CAL 1

Mix beans, water, and ham together. Bring to a boil, then turn to low and cook 2 hrs. Add carrots, then cook 1 hr.

WHOLE - 8 SERVINGS	1 SERVING
CAR = 161	CAR = 20
SOD = 2780	SOD = 348
CAL = 1525	CAL = 191

BEEF SOUP

- ☆ 6 cups water
- ☆ 1 lb. stewing beef = SOD 172, CAL 735
- ☆ 1 onion, chopped = CAR 10, SOD 3, CAL 48
- ☆ 1 c. beef broth (HOMEMADE) = 0
- ☆ 3 carrots, sliced = CAR 15, SOD 157, CAL 93
- ☆ 1 bay leaf = CAL 1
- ☆ 3 celery stalks, sliced = CAR 1, SOD 41, CAL 7
- ☆ 2 c. cabbage, chopped = CAR 6, SOD 32, CAL 43
- ☆ 4 mushrooms, sliced = CAR 1, SOD 2, CAL 9

Bring beef, water, onion, and bay leaf to a boil. Turn heat to low and simmer.

Cook until beef is cooked, about 1 to 2 hrs. Add broth, carrots, and celery. Cook 15 min. Add cabbage and mushrooms, cook 5 min. Remove bay leaf before serving.

WHOLE—4 SERVINGS	1 SERVING
CAR = 33	CAR = 8
SOD = 407	SOD = 102
CAL = 936	CAL = 234

HOMEMADE

BACON BITS

☆   8 slices bacon = SOD 760, CAL 400

Cook bacon until crisp, crumble. Store in refrigerator.

MAKES—1 CUP	½ CUP	¼ CUP
CAR = 0	CAR = 0	CAR = 0
SOD = 760	SOD = 380	SOD = 190
CAL = 400	CAL = 200	CAL = 100

BALSAMIC VINEGAR

☆   4 T. apple cider vinegar = 0

☆   2 t. sugar = CAR 8, CAL 33

Combine all ingredients. Shake well.

MAKES—4 T.	2 T.	1 T.	4 t.	2 t.	1 t.
CAR = 8	CAR = 4	CAR = 2	CAR = 1	CAR = 1	CAR = 1
SOD = 0	SOD = 1	SOD = 1	SOD = 1	SOD = 0	SOD = 0
CAL = 33	CAL = 17	CAL = 9	CAL = 6	CAL = 3	CAL = 2

BBQ SAUCE

☆ 1 c. honey (HOMEMADE) = CAR 1000, SOD 12, CAL 2872

☆ ¼ c. molasses = CAR 61, SOD 30, CAL 238

☆ 3 T. ketchup = CAR 15, SOD 480, CAL 60

☆ 1/8 t. cinnamon = CAR 1, CAL 1

☆ ½ t. paprika = CAR 1, SOD 1, CAL 3

☆ 1/8 t. ginger = CAL 1

☆ 1/8 t. pepper = CAL 1

☆ 1/8 t. oregano = CAL 1

☆ ¼ t. garlic, minced = CAL 1

☆ ¼ c. steak sauce (HOMEMADE) = CAR 18, SOD 591, CAL 76

☆ 2 T. Worcestershire sauce (HOMEMADE) = CAR 6, SOD 6, CAL 34

☆ 1 T. mustard = SOD 170, CAL 10

☆ 1 ½ c. brown sugar (HOMEMADE) = CAR 323, SOD 14, CAL 1248

Mix all ingredients together. Refrigerate.

MAKES—3 CUPS	2 ¼ CUPS	2 CUPS	1 ½ CUPS	1 CUP
CAR = 1303	CAR = 977	CAR = 869	CAR = 652	CAR = 434
SOD = 1304	SOD = 978	SOD = 869	SOD = 652	SOD = 435
CAL = 4546	CAL = 3410	CAL = 3031	CAL = 2273	CAL = 1515

2/3 CUP	½ CUP	¼ CUP	3 T.	2 T.
CAR = 290	CAR = 217	CAR = 109	CAR = 81	CAR = 54
SOD = 290	SOD = 217	SOD = 109	SOD = 82	SOD = 54
CAL = 1010	CAL = 4758	CAL = 505	CAL = 284	CAL = 189

BEEF BROTH

☆ 1 lb. beef bones

☆ 8 c. water

Boil bones in water for 6 hrs. Strain broth.

MAKES 6 CUPS

CAR = 0

SOD = 0

CAL = 0

BEEF GRAVY

- ☆ ½ c. drippings = CAR 1, SOD 18, CAL 10
- ☆ ½ c. flour = CAR 23, SOD 1, CAL 114
- ☆ 4 c. milk = CAR 48, SOD 412, CAL 334
- ☆ ¼ t. pepper to taste = CAL 1

Cook drippings and flour over medium heat, stirring for 5 to 10 min. until mixture starts to turn brown. Add pepper. Slowly add milk, stirring constantly until gravy boils and thickens.

MAKES 4 CUPS	2 ½ CUPS	2 CUPS	1 ½ CUPS	1 CUP
CAR = 72	CAR = 45	CAR = 36	CAR = 27	CAR = 18
SOD = 431	SOD = 269	SOD = 216	SOD = 162	SOD = 108
CAL = 459	CAL 287	CAL = 230	CAL = 172	CAL = 115

BISCUIT DOUGH

☆ 5 c. flour = CAR 371, SOD 13, CAL 2275

☆ 1 ½ c. sugar = CAR 300, SOD 3, CAL 1161

☆ 5 t. baking powder = CAR 7, SOD 2438, CAL 12

☆ 2 c. butter, cut into pieces = SOD 2908, CAL 3240

☆ 12 T. butter, melted = SOD 1092, CAL 1224

☆ 1 ½ c. buttermilk (HOMEMADE) = CAR 195, SOD 188, CAL 135

Mix flour, sugar, and baking powder together. Add 1 c. butter. Work batter with fingers until mixture resembles coarse meal and pea-sized pieces of butter remain. Add buttermilk. Knead until dough comes together.

MAKES 48 CT	20 CT	16 CT	12 CT	10 CT
CAR = 873	CAR = 364	CAR = 291	CAR = 218	CAR = 182
SOD = 6642	SOD = 2768	SOD = 2214	SOD = 1661	SOD = 1422
CAL = 8047	CAL = 3353	CAL = 2682	CAL = 2012	CAL = 1677

8 CT	5 CT	2 CT	1 CT
CAR = 146	CAR = 91	CAR = 36	CAR = 18
SOD = 1107	SOD = 692	SOD = 277	SOD = 138
CAL = 1341	CAL = 838	CAL = 335	CAL = 168

BREADCRUMBS

☆   24 slices of bread = CAR 192, SOD 2044, CAL 1104

Preheat the oven to 250 to 300 degrees F. Lay bread slices on a baking sheet in a single layer. Bake for about 15 minutes, turn the slices over, and bake for an additional 15 minutes. The bread should be perfectly crisp when you remove it from the oven. It should snap when you break up the pieces of bread. Place bread into either a mixer or a blender, and process until the breadcrumbs have an even, fine texture. Store your breadcrumbs in an airtight container in the freezer for up to six months. You don't need to let the breadcrumbs thaw before using.

MAKES 6 CUPS	5 CUPS	4 CUPS	2 CUPS	1½ CUPS
CAR = 288	CAR = 240	CAR = 192	CAR = 96	CAR = 72
SOD = 3066	SOD = 2555	SOD = 2044	SOD = 1022	SOD = 767
CAL = 1656	CAL = 1380	CAL = 1104	CAL = 552	CAL = 414
1¼ CUPS	**1 CUP**	**¾ CUP**	**½ CUP**	**3 T.**
CAR = 60	CAR = 48	CAR = 36	CAR = 24	CAR = 9
SOD = 639	SOD = 511	SOD = 383	SOD = 256	SOD = 96
CAL = 345	CAL = 276	CAL = 207	CAL = 138	CAL = 51
2 T.	**1 T.**			
CAR = 6	CAR = 3			
SOD = 64	SOD = 32			
CAL = 34	CAL = 17			

BROWN SUGAR

☆ 4 ¼ c. sugar = CAR 800, SOD 8, CAL 3096

☆ 4 ¼ T. molasses = CAR 60, SOD 30, CAL 232

Combine well.

MAKES 4 ½ CUPS	4 CUPS	2 ¼ CUPS	2 CUPS	1 ¾ CUPS	1 ½ CUPS
CAR = 968	CAR = 860	CAR = 484	CAR = 430	CAR = 376	CAR = 323
SOD = 43	SOD = 38	SOD = 21	SOD = 19	SOD = 17	SOD = 14
CAL = 3744	CAL = 3328	CAL = 1664	CAL = 1664	CAL 1456	CAL = 1248
1 1/3 CUPS	**1 CUP**	**12 T.**	**¾ CUP**	**2/3 CUP**	**½ CUP**
CAR = 287	CAR = 215	CAR = 161	CAR = 161	CAR = 143	CAR = 108
SOD = 13	SOD = 10	SOD = 7	SOD = 7	SOD = 6	SOD = 5
CAL = 1109	CAL = 832	CAL = 624	CAL = 624	CAL = 555	CAL = 416
8 T.	**6 T.**	**1/3 CUP**	**5 T.**	**¼ CUP**	**4 T.**
CAR = 108	CAR = 81	CAR = 72	CAR = 68	CAR = 54	CAR = 54
SOD = 5	SOD = 3	SOD = 3	SOD = 3	SOD = 3	SOD = 3
CAL = 416	CAL = 312	CAL = 277	CAL = 260	CAL = 208	CAL = 208
3 T.	**2 T.**	**1/8 CUP**	**4 ½ t.**	**1 T.**	**½ T.**
CAR = 39	CAR = 27	CAR = 27	CAR = 20	CAR = 13	CAR = 9
SOD = 3	SOD = 1	SOD = 1	SOD = 1	SOD = 1	SOD = 1
CAL = 156	CAL 104	CAL = 104	CAL = 78	CAL = 52	CAL = 26
2 t.	**1 t.**				
CAR = 4	CAR = 2				
SOD = 0	SOD = 0				
CAL = 17	CAL = 9				

CHICKEN BROTH

☆ 1 lb. chicken bones

☆ 8 c. water

Boil bones in water for 6 hrs. Strain broth.

MAKES 6 CUPS

CAR = 0

SOD = 0

CAL = 0

CONDENSED CREAM OF SOUP

☆ 2 c. cold milk = CAR 24, SOD 206, CAL 167

☆ 4 T. cornstarch = CAR 28, CAL 120

☆ 3 T. butter = SOD 273, CAL 306

☆ 2 t. chicken bouillon = CAR 1, SOD 743, CAL 11

☆ ¼ t. black pepper = CAL 1

☆ ½ t. onion powder = CAR 1, SOD 1, CAL 4

☆ ½ t. garlic powder = CAR 1, SOD 1, CAL 5

☆ ¼ t. dried parsley = SOD 1

In a small saucepan, whisk together milk and cornstarch. Add butter, bouillon, pepper, onion powder, garlic powder, and parsley. Bring to a boil, stirring frequently. Once boiling, simmer for 30 more seconds to thicken. (Use in recipes to replace two 10.75-oz. cans of cream of (anything) soup.)

MAKES 2 ½ CUPS	1 ¼ CUP
CAR = 60	CAR = 30
SOD = 1225	SOD = 613
CAL = 614	CAL = 307

CONDENSED CREAM OF MUSHROOM SOUP

☆ Stir in 2 4-oz. cans of mushroom pieces for 2 cans of soup = CAR 12, SOD 1940, CAL 116

☆ Stir in 1 4-oz. can of mushroom pieces for 1 can of soup = CAR 6, SOD 970, CAL 58

3 CUPS = 2 CANS	1½ CUPS = 1 CAN
CAR = 72	CAR = 36
SOD = 3165	SOD = 1583
CAL = 730	CAL = 365

CONDENSED CREAM OF CHICKEN SOUP

☆ Stir in ½ c. of shredded chicken for 2 cans of soup = CAR 0, SOD 52, CAL 116

☆ Stir in ¼ c. of shredded chicken for 1 can of soup = CAR 0, SOD 26, CAL 58

3 CUPS = 2 CANS	1½ CUPS = 1 CAN
CAR = 60	CAR = 30
SOD = 1280	SOD = 639
CAL = 730	CAL = 365

CONDENSED CREAM OF CELERY SOUP

☆ Stir in ½ c. of sautéed chopped celery for 2 cans of soup = CAR 2, SOD 68, CAL 14

☆ Stir in ¼ c. of sautéed chopped celery for 1 can of soup = CAR 1, SOD 34, CAL 7

3 CUPS = 2 CANS	1½ CUPS = 1 CAN
CAR = 62	CAR = 31
SOD = 1293	SOD = 647
CAL = 628	CAL = 314

CONDENSED CHEDDAR CHEESE SOUP

☆ Stir in ½ c. of shredded cheddar cheese for 2 cans of soup =
CAR 0, SOD 351, CAL 228

☆ Stir in ¼ c. of shredded cheddar cheese for 1 can of soup =
CAR 0, SOD 175, CAL 114

3 CUPS = 2 CANS	1 ½ CUPS = 1 CAN
CAR = 60	CAR = 30
SOD = 1576	SOD = 788
CAL = 842	CAL = 421

CONDENSED ONION SOUP

☆ Stir in ½ c. of sautéed onion for 2 cans of soup = CAR 9, SOD 3, CAL 46

☆ Stir in ¼ c. of sautéed onion for 1 can of soup = CAR 5, SOD 2, CAL 23

3 CUPS = 2 CANS	1½ CUPS = 1 CAN
CAR = 69	CAR = 35
SOD = 1228	SOD = 615
CAL = 660	CAL = 330

CONDENSED TOMATO SOUP

☆ Stir in ½ c. of diced tomatoes for 2 cans of soup = CAR 2, SOD 130, CAL 20

☆ Stir in ¼ c. of diced tomatoes for 1 can of soup = CAR 1, SOD 65, CAL 10

☆ (IF SMOOTH SOUP IS WANTED, PUREE TOMATOES BEFORE ADDING)

3 CUPS = 2 CANS	1 ½ CUPS = 1 CAN
CAR = 62	CAR = 31
SOD = 1355	SOD = 678
CAL = 634	CAL = 317

DRY RANCH DRESSING MIX

☆ ½ c. dried parsley = CAR 1, SOD 58, CAL 38

☆ 1 t. garlic powder = CAR 2, SOD 2, CAL 10

☆ 4 T. onion flakes = CAR 15, SOD 4, CAL 70

☆ 1 t. paprika = SOD 2, CAL 6

☆ 1 t. onion powder = CAR 2, SOD 2, CAL 8

☆ ½ t. cayenne pepper = CAR 1, CAL 3

Combine well.

(4 T. EQUALS 1 PACKAGE)

MAKES 4 T.

CAR = 21

SOD = 72

CAL = 135

ENCHILADA SAUCE

- ☆ ½ c. onion, chopped = CAR 7, SOD 2, CAL 24
- ☆ 3 T. garlic, minced = 0
- ☆ 3 T. chili powder = CAR 5, SOD 227, CAL 71
- ☆ 1 T. cumin = 0
- ☆ 2 c. tomato sauce (HOMEMADE) = CAR 49, SOD 88, CAL 1019
- ☆ 1 c. water

Place all ingredients in a blender. Blend until smooth. It will be thick. You can add more water if you like thinner sauce. Place in a jar with lid and store for up to a week in the refrigerator.

MAKES 3 CUPS	2 ½ CUPS	1 ¼ CUP
CAR = 61	CAR = 51	CAR = 25
SOD = 317	SOD = 264	SOD = 132
CAL = 1114	CAL = 928	CAL = 464

FAJITA SEASONING MIX

☆ ¼ t. garlic powder = CAL 2

☆ ½ t. onion powder = CAR 1, SOD 1, CAL 4

☆ ¼ t. cayenne pepper = CAL 1

☆ 1 T. chili powder = CAR 2, SOD 76, CAL 24

☆ 1 t. cornstarch = CAR 2, CAL 9

☆ 1 t. paprika = CAR 1, SOD 1, CAL 6

☆ 1 ½ t. cumin = 0

Combine all ingredients well.

(8 t. EQUALS 1 PACKAGE)

MAKES 8 t.	4 t.
CAR = 7	CAR = 4
SOD = 78	SOD = 39
CAL = 46	CAL = 23

HALF-AND-HALF

☆   4 c. milk = CAR 24, SOD 412, CAL 334

☆   4 T. melted butter = SOD 364, CAL 408

Combine and mix well.

MAKES 4 CUPS	3 ½ CUPS	3 CUPS	2 ¼ CUPS	2 CUPS
CAR = 24	CAR = 21	CAR = 18	CAR = 14	CAR = 12
SOD = 776	SOD = 679	SOD = 582	SOD = 437	SOD = 388
CAL = 442	CAL = 387	CAL = 332	CAL = 249	CAL = 221
1 ½ CUPS	1 CUP	¾ CUP	½ CUP	¼ CUP
CAR = 9	CAR = 6	CAR = 5	CAR = 3	CAR = 2
SOD = 291	SOD = 194	SOD = 146	SOD = 97	SOD = 49
CAL = 166	CAL = 111	CAL = 83	CAL = 55	CAL = 28
2 T.	1 T.			
CAR = 1	CAR = 0			
SOD = 24	SOD = 12			
CAL = 14	CAL = 7			

HEAVY CREAM

☆ 5 ¾ c. milk = CAR 27, SOD 232, CAL 188

☆ 2 ½ c. melted butter = SOD 1454, CAL 1620

Combine and mix well.

MAKES 5 CUPS	4 CUPS	3 CUPS	2 CUPS	1 ¾ CUPS
CAR = 45	CAR = 36	CAR = 27	CAR = 18	CAR = 16
SOD = 2810	SOD = 2248	SOD = 1686	SOD = 1124	SOD = 984
CAL = 3015	CAL = 2412	CAL = 1809	CAL = 1206	CAL = 1055
1 ½ CUPS	1 CUP	¾ CUP	2/3 CUP	½ CUP
CAR = 14	CAR = 9	CAR = 7	CAR = 6	CAR = 5
SOD = 843	SOD = 562	SOD = 422	SOD = 375	SOD = 281
CAL = 905	CAL = 603	CAL = 452	CAL = 402	CAL = 302
1/3 CUP	¼ CUP	4 T.	2 T.	1 T.
CAR = 3	CAR = 2	CAR = 2	CAR = 1	CAR = 1
SOD = 187	SOD = 141	SOD = 141	SOD = 70	SOD = 35
CAL = 201	CAL = 151	CAL = 151	CAL = 75	CAL = 38
1 t.				
CAR = 0				
SOD = 12				
CAL = 13				

HONEY (SUBSTITUTE)

☆ 2 ½ c. sugar = CAR 1000, SOD 12, CAL 3872

☆ ½ c. water

Combine well.

MAKES 1 CUP	2/3 CUP	½ CUP	1/3 CUP	¼ CUP
CAR = 1000	CAR = 667	CAR = 500	CAR = 333	CAR = 250
SOD = 12	SOD = 8	SOD = 6	SOD = 4	SOD = 3
CAL = 3872	CAL = 2581	CAL = 1936	CAL = 1291	CAL = 968
4 T.	**3 T.**	**2 T.**	**1½ T.**	**1 T.**
CAR = 250	CAR = 188	CAR = 125	CAR = 94	CAR = 63
SOD = 3	SOD = 2	SOD = 2	SOD = 1	SOD = 1
CAL 968	CAL = 726	CAL = 484	CAL = 363	CAL = 242
½ T.				
CAR = 32				
SOD = 1				
CAL = 121				

HONEY-GLAZED CARROTS

☆ 3 T. butter = SOD 273, CAL 306

☆ ½ onion, diced = CAR 10, SOD 3, CAL 24

☆ ½ c. chicken broth = 0

☆ 3 ½ c. sliced carrots, cooked = CAR 30, SOD 309, CAL 184

☆ ¼ c. honey (HOMEMADE) = CAR 250, SOD 3, CAL 968

☆ ¼ t. pepper = CAR 1, SOD 1, CAL 2

☆ 1 T. honey (HOMEMADE) = CAR 63, SOD 1, CAL 242

☆ 1 T. fresh parsley = SOD 1

Preheat oven to 400°. Melt butter in cast-iron pan over medium-high heat. Toss the onions in the pan and cook for about 5 min., stirring occasionally. The onions should be translucent after about 5 minutes. Add the broth to the pan, cook over medium heat for about 3 min. Toss the carrots in the pan, stir, then drizzle with ¼ cup honey. Add pepper. Carefully place the cast-iron pan in the preheated oven. Cook 25 to 30 min. Drizzle another T. of honey over top of the carrots, then stir. Transfer to a large serving bowl. Add garnish.

MAKES 4 CUPS	2 ½ CUPS
CAR = 354	CAR = 221
SOD = 591	SOD = 369
CAL = 1726	CAL = 1079

ITALIAN SEASONING MIX

☆ ¼ c. dried basil = CAR 2, SOD 14, CAL 42

☆ 2 T. dried thyme = CAR 1, SOD 3, CAL 15

☆ 2 T. dried marjoram = CAR 1, SOD 3, CAL 9

☆ 2 T. dried rosemary = CAR 1, SOD 3, CAL 22

☆ 2 T. dried oregano = CAR 1, SOD 2, CAL 16

☆ 2 t. garlic powder = CAR 4, SOD 4, CAL 21

☆ 2 T. dried coriander = CAR 1, SOD 4, CAL 30

☆ 1 t. sugar = CAR 4, CAL 16

Combine and mix well.

(4 T. EQUALS 1 PACKAGE)

MAKES 12 T.	4 T.	1 T.	2 t.	1½ t.
CAR = 15	CAR = 5	CAR = 1	CAR = 1	CAR = 1
SOD = 33	SOD = 11	SOD = 3	SOD = 2	SOD = 1
CAL = 171	CAL = 57	CAL = 14	CAL = 10	CAL = 7

1 t.	½ t.	¼ t.
CAR = 0	CAR = 0	CAR = 0
SOD = 1	SOD = 1	SOD = 1
CAL = 5	CAL = 3	CAL = 2

LEMON CONFIT (CURD)

☆ 5 T. sugar = CAR 60, CAL 232

☆ 6 lemons cut into ¼ = CAR 23, SOD 7, CAL 101

Pour some sugar into a mason jar. Layer lemons in jar, putting sugar mixture between lemons. Refrigerate 2 wks.

MAKES 2 CUPS	1 ¼ CUP	½ CUP
CAR = 83	CAR = 52	CAR = 21
SOD = 7	SOD = 4	SOD = 2
CAL = 333	CAL = 208	CAL = 83

MASTER MIX (BISQUICK)

- ☆ 8 c. flour = CAR 736, SOD 20, CAL 3640
- ☆ ¼ c. baking powder = CAR 15, SOD 5851, CAL 29
- ☆ 1 ½ c. dry milk = CAR 15, SOD 158, CAL 101
- ☆ 1 ½ c. butter = SOD 2181, CAL 2430

Sift together 4 c. flour and baking powder. Stir in dry milk. Cut in butter with 2 knives, until it looks like coarse cornmeal. Sift in remaining flour. Stir well.

Store in covered container at room temp.

MAKES 8 CUPS	4 CUPS	3 ½ CUPS	3 CUPS	2 ½ CUPS
CAR = 766	CAR = 383	CAR = 335	CAR = 287	CAR = 239
SOD = 8210	SOD = 4105	SOD = 3592	SOD = 3079	SOD = 2566
CAL = 6200	CAL = 3100	CAL = 2713	CAL = 2325	CAL = 1938

2 CUPS	1 ½ CUPS	1 ¼ CUPS	1 CUP	½ CUP
CAR = 192	CAR = 144	CAR = 120	CAR = 96	CAR = 48
SOD = 2053	SOD = 1539	SOD = 1283	SOD = 1026	SOD = 513
CAL = 1163	CAL = 1163	CAL = 969	CAL = 775	CAL = 388

RAISIN COOKIE DOUGH

☆ 1 c. oatmeal = CAR 46, SOD 5, CAL 307

☆ ¾ c. flour = CAR 69, SOD 2, CAL 341

☆ 1 ½ t. baking powder = CAR 2, SOD 731, CAL 4

☆ 1 ½ t. ground cinnamon = CAR 1, CAL 10

☆ 2 T. butter, melted and cooled slightly = SOD 182, CAL 204

☆ 1 large egg, room temperature = SOD 71, CAL 72

☆ 1 t. vanilla extract = CAR 1, CAL 12

☆ ½ c. honey (HOMEMADE) = CAR 500, SOD 6, CAL 1936

☆ ¼ c. raisins = CAR 28, SOD 4, CAL 108

Whisk together the oats, flour, baking powder, and cinnamon in a medium bowl. In a separate bowl, whisk together the butter, egg, and vanilla. Stir in honey. Add in flour mixture, stirring just until incorporated. Fold in raisins. Chill the cookie dough for 30 minutes.

MAKES 3 CUPS

CAR = 647

SOD = 841

CAL = 2816

SC PASTA SAUCE

☆ 2 c. mushrooms, sliced = CAR 3, SOD 7, CAL 31

☆ 3 t. garlic, minced = CAR 3, SOD 1, CAL 12

☆ 3 ½ c. tomatoes, diced = CAR 17, SOD 32, CAL 113

☆ 2 c. tomato sauce (HOMEMADE) = CAR 49, SOD 88, CAL 1019

☆ 1 T. basil = SOD 3, CAL 10

☆ 1 t. oregano = CAR 1, CAL 3

☆ 1 T. sugar = CAR 13, CAL 49

☆ ½ t. pepper = CAR 1, CAL 3

Cook mushrooms and garlic over medium heat for about 10 min. Place mixture into slow cooker. Add tomatoes, tomato sauce, basil, oregano, sugar, and pepper. Cook on low for 8 to 9 hrs.

MAKES 8 CUPS	6 CUPS	3 ¼ CUPS	3 CUPS	2 CUPS
CAR = 87	CAR = 65	CAR = 35	CAR = 33	CAR = 22
SOD = 256	SOD = 192	SOD = 104	SOD = 96	SOD = 64
CAL = 1240	CAL = 930	CAL = 504	CAL = 465	CAL = 310

1 ¾ CUPS	1 ½ CUPS	1 CUP	5 T.
CAR = 19	CAR = 16	CAR = 11	CAR = 4
SOD = 56	SOD = 48	SOD = 32	SOD = 12
CAL = 271	CAL = 233	CAL = 155	CAL = 58

PIZZA CRUST DOUGH

☆ 1 ¼ c. warm water

☆ 1 package yeast = CAR 1, SOD 4, CAL 23

☆ 1 t. sugar = CAR 4, CAL 16

☆ 1 T. olive oil = CAL 119

☆ 3 ½ c. flour = CAR 322, SOD 9, CAL 1593

☆ 2 t. cornmeal = CAR 80, SOD 7, CAL 387

Place ¼ c. warm water in large bowl. Sprinkle yeast over water. Stir in sugar.

Let stand 5 min. Add remaining water and oil. Stir in flour until dough pulls away from side of bowl. Put dough on lightly floured surface. Knead until smooth, 8 to 10 min. Coat large bowl with cooking spray. Put dough in bowl and roll to grease all sides. Cover loosely with plastic wrap. Let rise in warm place until almost doubled, about 45 min. Punch down dough. Coat 2 pizza pans with cooking spray. Sprinkle pans with cornmeal. Divide dough in half.

Roll dough out to fit pans. Put dough in pans and press against edge to form rim. Bake crust @ 450° for 10 min. Remove crust.

MAKES 2 CRUSTS	1 CRUST
CAR = 330	CAR = 165
SOD = 13	SOD = 7
CAL = 1763	CAL = 882

RANCH DRESSING

☆   1 t. garlic powder = CAR 2, SOD 2, CAL 10

☆   1 t. onion powder = CAR 2, SOD 2, CAL 8

☆   ½ t. pepper = CAL 3

☆   2 t. dried parsley = SOD 4, CAL 2

☆   ½ c. mayonnaise = SOD 698, CAL 748

☆   2/3 c. sour cream = CAR 4, SOD 72, CAL 296

☆   2 c. buttermilk (HOMEMADE) = CAR 24, SOD 207, CAL 174

Combine all of the ingredients in a jar with a tight-fitting lid. Shake until the mixture is well combined. Store the dressing in the refrigerator for up to 2 weeks. Shake before using.

MAKES 2 CUPS	1 CUP	¼ CUP
CAR = 32	CAR = 16	CAR = 4
SOD = 985	SOD = 493	SOD = 123
CAL = 1241	CAL = 621	CAL = 155

SALSA

☆ 7 c. stewed tomatoes = CAR 112, SOD 4620, CAL 630

☆ 1 onion, finely diced = CAR 10, SOD 3, CAL 48

☆ 2 t. minced garlic = 0

☆ 1 t. lime juice = CAL 1

☆ ½ c. canned sliced green chili = CAR 2, SOD 276, CAL 15

☆ 6 t. chopped fresh cilantro = SOD 3, CAL 2

Combine the tomatoes, onion, garlic, lime juice, green chili, and cilantro in a blender or food processor. Blend on low to desired smoothness.

MAKES 2 CUPS	2 ½ CUPS	1 CUP	½ CUP	1/3 CUP
CAR = 124	CAR = 93	CAR = 62	CAR = 31	CAR = 21
SOD = 4902	SOD = 3677	SOD = 2451	SOD = 1226	SOD = 817
CAL = 2241	CAL = 1681	CAL = 1121	CAL = 560	CAL = 374

¼ CUP	3 T.	1 T.
CAR = 16	CAR = 9	CAR = 3
SOD = 613	SOD = 408	SOD = 136
CAL = 280	CAL = 186	CAL = 62

SEASONED BREADCRUMBS

- ☆ 16 slices of bread = CAR 192, SOD 2044, CAL 1104
- ☆ 4 t. dried parsley = CAR 2, SOD 10, CAL 6
- ☆ 4 t. dried basil = SOD 4, CAL 14
- ☆ 4 t. dried oregano = SOD 2, CAL 10
- ☆ 4 t. dried thyme = SOD 2, CAL 12
- ☆ 4 t. garlic powder = CAR 4, SOD 8, CAL 42
- ☆ ¼ t. pepper = CAL 1

Preheat the oven to 250°. Lay bread slices on a baking sheet in a single layer. Bake for about 15 min., then turn the slices over and bake for an additional 15 min. The bread should be perfectly crisp when you remove it from the oven. It should snap when you break up the pieces of bread. Place bread into either a mixer or blender and add spices and process until the breadcrumbs have an even, fine texture. Store in an airtight container in the freezer for up to six months.

MAKES 4 CUPS	1 CUP	½ CUP	¼ CUP
CAR = 192	CAR = 48	CAR = 24	CAR = 12
SOD = 2044	SOD = 511	SOD = 256	SOD = 128
CAL = 1104	CAL = 276	CAL = 138	CAL = 69

SOY SAUCE

☆   2 c. beef broth (HOMEMADE) = 0

☆   4 T. balsamic vinegar (HOMEMADE) = CAR 8, CAL 33

☆   4 t. cider vinegar = 0

☆   2 T. molasses = CAR 29, SOD 15, CAL 116

☆   2 t. molasses = CAR 4, SOD 2, CAL 19

☆   pinch of white pepper = CAL 1

☆   pinch of garlic powder = CAR 1, CAL 2

☆   pinch of ground ginger = CAL 1

Place all ingredients in a small pot. Bring mixture to a gentle simmer (small bubbles should just break on the surface) and simmer until reduced to about 4 c. Pour into a tight-sealing jar and refrigerate up to 10 days.

MAKES 4 CUPS	2 CUPS	1 CUP	½ CUP	6 T.
CAR = 39	CAR = 20	CAR = 10	CAR = 5	CAR = 4
SOD = 17	SOD = 9	SOD = 4	SOD = 2	SOD = 2
CAL = 172	CAL = 86	CAL = 43	CAL = 22	CAL = 16

1/3 CUP	¼ CUP	3 T.	2 T.	1 T.
CAR = 3	CAR = 2	CAR = 2	CAR = 1	CAR = 1
SOD = 1	SOD = 1	SOD = 0	SOD = 0	SOD = 0
CAL = 14	CAL = 14	CAL = 8	CAL = 5	CAR = 3

2 t.	1½ t.
CAR = 0	CAR = 0
SOD = 0	SOD = 0
CAL = 0	CAL = 1

STEAK SAUCE

☆ 1 ¼ c. ketchup = CAR 100, SOD 3200, CAL 400

☆ 2 T. mustard = CAR 1, SOD 341, CAL 20

☆ 2 T. Worcestershire sauce (HOMEMADE) = CAR 5, SOD 5, CAL 24

☆ 1 ½ T. cider vinegar = SOD 1, CAL 5

☆ ½ t. pepper = CAR 1, CAL 3

Mix all ingredients together. Refrigerate.

MAKES 1 ½ CUPS	1 T.	2 t.
CAR = 107	CAR = 5	CAR = 3
SOD = 3547	SOD = 148	SOD = 99
CAL = 452	CAL = 19	CAL = 13

TOMATO SAUCE

- ☆ 6 lb. tomatoes = CAR 74, SOD 136, CAL 490
- ☆ 1 T. garlic, minced = 0
- ☆ 1/3 c. olive oil = CAL 1262
- ☆ ½ c. basil = CAR 24, SOD 39, CAL 285
- ☆ pepper to taste = CAL 1

Preheat oven to 250°. Place tomatoes on large baking sheet with a raised 1-inch lip. Add garlic and drizzle with olive oil. Use your fingers to mix well to coat. Top with basil and season with pepper. Bake 4 hrs. or until tomatoes are soft and bursting. Allow to cool, then pour into a blender in batches. Pulse 2 to 3 times, then blend for 1 minute or until desired chunkiness. Pour into quart jars or pour into freezer bags to freeze flat. It will keep in the refrigerator for 1 week or in the freezer for 4 months.

MAKES 2 QUARTS	4 CUPS	2 CUPS	1 CUP	½ CUP
CAR = 98	CAR = 98	CAR = 49	CAR = 25	CAR = 12
SOD = 175	SOD = 175	SOD = 88	SOD = 44	SOD = 22
CAL = 2038	CAL = 2038	CAL = 1019	CAL = 510	CAL = 255

TORTILLA MIX

☆ 16 c. flour = CAR 92, SOD 3, CAL 455

☆ 2 T. baking powder = CAR 8, SOD 2926, CAL 15

☆ ½ c. shortening = SOD 4, CAL 906

Combine and mix well. Store in airtight container.

MAKES 16 CUPS	4 CUPS	2 CUPS
CAR = 100	CAR = 25	CAR = 13
SOD = 2930	SOD = 733	SOD = 366
CAL = 1376	CAL = 344	CAL = 172

TORTILLAS

☆   4 c. tortilla mix (HOMEMADE) = CAR 25, SOD 733, CAL 344

☆   1 ¼ c. warm water

☆   2 c. flour = CAR 184, SOD 5, CAL 910

Place 2 c. tortilla mix in a bowl, making a well in the center. Add ½ to ¾ c. warm water, a little at a time, mixing until you have a soft dough. Knead dough for a short time till it becomes elastic. Cover with plastic and let it rest for 10 to 15 min. Form 16 small balls, pull the dough around the bottom of the ball to make top smooth. Set aside, covered with plastic wrap. Dip dough balls in flour and roll out thinly. Cook on preheated dry griddle until top begins to bubble, flip and cook for about 15 seconds more. To keep warm, stack between towels. Wrap in plastic wrap and store in the refrigerator.

MAKES 32 TORTILLAS	20 TORTILLAS	18 TORTILLAS	16 TORTILLAS
CAR = 209	CAR = 131	CAR = 118	CAR = 105
SOD = 738	SOD = 461	SOD = 415	SOD = 369
CAL = 1254	CAL = 784	CAL = 705	CAL = 627
12 TORTILLAS	10 TORTILLAS	8 TORTILLAS	7 TORTILLAS
CAR = 78	CAR = 65	CAR = 52	CAR = 46
SOD = 277	SOD = 231	SOD = 185	SOD = 160
CAL = 470	CAL = 392	CAL = 314	CAL = 274
6 TORTILLAS	4 TORTILLAS	1 TORTILLA	
CAR = 39	CAR = 26	CAR = 7	
SOD = 138	SOD = 92	SOD = 23	
CAL = 235	CAL = 157	CAL = 39	

WHIPPED TOPPING

☆ 3 c. heavy cream (HOMEMADE) = CAR 27, SOD 1686, CAL 1808

☆ 6 T. powdered sugar = CAR 48, CAL 186

☆ ¾ t. vanilla = CAL 9

Combine all ingredients. Mix until stiff peaks form.

MAKES 3 CUPS	2 CUPS	1½ CUPS	1 CUP	¾ CUP
CAR = 75	CAR = 50	CAR = 38	CAR = 25	CAR = 19
SOD = 1686	SOD = 1124	SOD = 843	SOD = 562	SOD = 422
CAL = 2003	CAL = 1335	CAL = 1002	CAL = 668	CAL = 501

2/3 CUP	½ CUP	¼ CUP
CAR = 17	CAR = 13	CAR = 6
SOD = 375	SOD = 281	SOD = 141
CAL = 445	CAL = 334	CAL = 167

WORCESTERSHIRE SAUCE

☆ ½ c. apple cider vinegar = CAR 1, SOD 6, CAL 25

☆ 2 T. soy sauce (HOMEMADE) = CAR 2, CAL 10

☆ 2 T. water

☆ 1 T. brown sugar (HOMEMADE) = CAR 13, SOD 1, CAL 52

☆ ¼ t. ginger = CAL 2

☆ ¼ t. dried mustard = SOD 14, CAL 1

☆ ¼ t. garlic powder = CAR 1, CAL 3

☆ 1/8 t. cinnamon = CAR 1, CAL 1

☆ 1/8 t. black pepper = CAL 1

Place all the ingredients in a medium pot and stir to combine. Bring mixture to a boil, constantly stirring. Simmer for a minute, then remove and cool. Store in the refrigerator. Shake well before using.

MAKES ½ CUP	¼ CUP	3 T.	2 T.	1 T.
CAR = 22	CAR = 11	CAR = 8	CAR = 6	CAR = 3
SOD = 21	SOD = 11	SOD = 8	SOD = 5	SOD = 3
CAL = 95	CAL = 48	CAL = 36	CAL = 24	CAL = 12

2 t.	1½ t.	1 t.	¼ t.
CAR = 2	CAR = 2	CAR = 1	CAR = 0
SOD = 2	SOD-2	SOD = 1	SOD = 0
CAL = 8	CAL = 6	CAL = 4	CAL = 1

CPSIA information can be obtained
at www.ICGtesting.com
Printed in the USA
BVHW011533170422
634491BV00003B/84